Italian & Pasta

Publisher & Creative Director: Nick Wells
Senior Editor: Cat Emslie
Layouts: Basil UK Ltd
Production and Digital Design: Chris Herbert
Production Director: Claire Walker
With thanks to: Gina Steer

This is a **FLAME TREE** Book

FLAME TREE PUBLISHING
Crabtree Hall, Crabtree Lane
Fulham, London SW6 6TY
United Kingdom
www.flametreepublishing.com

Flame Tree is part of The Foundry Creative Media Company Limited

First published 2007

ISBN: 978-1-84451-952-1

A copy of the CIP data for this book is available from the British Library.

Printed in China

Italian & Pasta

Quick and Easy, Proven Recipes

FLAME TREE
PUBLISHING

Contents

Contents

Meats 124

Poultry & Game

Contents

Vegetables & Salads

Entertaining & Desserts

Essential Ingredients

Owing to the cuisine's popularity, basic Italian storecupboard ingredients are commonplace items on supermarket shelves. Even fresh ingredients that used to be difficult to find are available all year round, often in parts of the world where previously they were unheard of. For those who enjoy Italian food and cooking this is good news – delicious, authentic Italian cuisine can now be enjoyed anywhere and at any time.

Cheese

Dolcelatte This cheese, which translates as 'sweet milk', comes from the Lombardy region. Dolcelatte is a creamy, blue cheese and has a luscious, sweet taste. It is very soft and melts in the mouth, often appealing to those who find more traditional blue cheeses, like Roquefort and Gorgonzola, too strongly flavoured.

Fontina This is a dense, smooth and slightly elastic cheese with a straw-coloured interior. Fontina is made in the Valle d'Aosta region and has a delicate nutty flavour with a hint of mild honey. It is often served melted in which case the flavour becomes very earthy.

Gorgonzola This is a traditional blue cheese from the Lombardy region. Made from cow's milk, the cheese has a sharp, spicy flavour as well as being rich and creamy.

Ricotta When cheese is made, the solids in the milk are separated from the liquid by coagulation, however, some solids are always lost to the whey. To retrieve these solids, the milk is heated until they come to the surface. They then are  skimmed off and drained in woven baskets until the curd is solid enough to stick together. The resulting cheese is ricotta (literally meaning 'recooked'). Good-quality ricotta should be firm but not solid and consist of fine, delicate grains. Ricotta is used in both savoury and sweet dishes.

Mozzarella di Bufala Mozzarella is a fresh cheese, prized more for its texture than its flavour which is really quite bland. It melts beautifully, however, on pizzas and in pasta dishes, and is also good served cold in salads. It is usually sold in tubs along with its whey and should have a floppy rather than a rubbery texture. The fresher it is when eaten, the better.

Parmigiano-Reggiano One of the world's finest cheeses, Parmigiano-Reggiano is also one of the most versatile cooking cheeses. Its production is very carefully regulated to guarantee a consistent high-quality result. The trademark is branded all over the rind, so that even a small piece is easily identified. Buy it in pieces, rather than ready-grated.

Pecorino This is the generic term for cheeses made purely from sheep's milk. All Pecorino cheeses are excellent for grating or shaving on to both hot and cold dishes. Each type of Pecorino is characteristic of a particular region and a particular breed of sheep. Pecorino Romano is made in the countryside around Rome between November and late June. Pecorino Sardo is made in Sardinia and Pecorino Toscano comes from Tuscany and tends to mature younger than other Pecorino cheeses.

Mascarpone Technically, mascarpone is not a cheese but a by-product obtained from making Parmesan. A culture is added to the cream that has been skimmed off the milk that was used to make the cheese. This is then gently heated and allowed to mature and thicken. Mascarpone is most famous as the main ingredient in Tiramisu, but it is a very versatile ingredient and is used in all sorts of sweet and savoury recipes.

Cured Meats

Coppa This boned shoulder of pork is rolled and cured with salt, pepper and nutmeg and then aged for about three months. It has a flavour not unlike prosciutto but contains equal amounts of fat and lean. It is excellent for larding the breasts of game birds, adding both fat and flavour, or for wrapping leaner types of meats.

Pancetta Essentially, pancetta is Italian streaky bacon but its depth of flavour is unrivalled by ordinary bacon. It is often flavoured with herbs, cloves, nutmeg, garlic, salt and pepper and sometimes fennel seeds – it is then often air-dried. It is also available smoked. Use it in slices or cut into lardons.

Prosciutto There are many types of cured ham available, but the two best types are Prosciutto di San Daniele and Prosciutto di Parma. The first comes from the Friuli region where the pigs feed in the fields and oak woods, accounting for the leanness of the meat. The second type, also known as Parma ham or prosciutto crudo, is made from pigs that have been fed on local grain as well as the whey left over from the making of Parmigiano-Reggiano. This meat is usually fattier.

Salami Italy produces a huge range of salamis, each with its own local character. The one most commonly available in Britain is probably Milano salami which comes sliced in packets or in one piece from major supermarkets.

Vegetables and Herbs

Artichokes Very popular in Italian cooking, artichokes are available in many different varieties and forms: from tiny, young artichokes cooked and eaten whole to enormous globe artichokes, prized for their meaty hearts which can be sliced, stuffed or grilled. Artichokes are often cooked and preserved and served as an antipasto, on pizzas or in pasta dishes.

Aubergines These vegetables are popular all over the Mediterranean, probably because of their affinity with olive oil and garlic. In Britain, aubergines tend to be fatter and somewhat juicier than the Mediterranean varieties which are often elongated and marked with bright purple streaks.

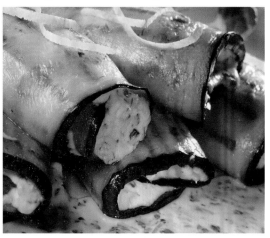

Broad Beans Fresh broad beans are a prized early-summer speciality and in Italy are eaten raw with pecorino cheese. As the season pro-gresses, they are best cooked and peeled as they tend to become coarse and grainy.

Cavallo Nero A member of the cabbage family, cavallo nero has long, slender, very ridged leaves which are dark green in colour. It has a strong but rather sweet cabbage flavour. Large supermarkets stock it in season, but if it is unavailable, use Savoy cabbage instead.

Garlic Garlic is one of the most important flavours in Italian cooking. When buying garlic, check it carefully – the heads should be firm without soft spots. Look for fresh, green garlic in spring.

Herbs A number of fresh herbs are used in Italian cooking but the most important ones are basil, parsley, rosemary, sage, marjoram and oregano. These are all widely used herbs and are available from most supermarkets but are also very easy to grow, even on a windowsill.

Lemons Italian lemons tend to be a little sweeter than the ones available in Britain. They are an essential flavour in many Italian dishes, especially seafood and sweet dishes.

Pumpkins and Squashes Often overlooked in Britain, pumpkins and the many varieties of squash are widely used in Italian cooking. They are excellent for enriching stews – some varieties have flesh which breaks down during cooking.

They are also used for risottos and pasta fillings. Pumpkins and squashes have an affinity with prosciutto, sage, pine nuts, Parmesan cheese and mostardo di cremona.

Rocket This peppery salad leaf has become popular in recent years and is now very easy to find. It is known by many other names including rucola, rughetta, arugula and roquette. It does not keep well.

Tomatoes Tomatoes are another essential flavour in Italian recipes. Unfortunately, British tomatoes tend not to be as good as their Italian counter-parts. It is best to use tomatoes only in season and, at other times, to use good-quality, tinned Italian tomatoes.

Wild Mushrooms Mushroom hunting is a very popular and lucrative business in Italy, so much so that there are strict regulations regarding the minimum size for picking mushrooms. Many excellent edible varieties of wild mushrooms grow in Britain, but it is vital to seek expert advice before picking them on your own as some varieties are poisonous. Many large supermarkets now sell varieties of wild mushrooms in season but they tend to be expensive.

Bread

Italian breads tend to be coarser and more open-textured than British breads. They are made with unbleached flours and are left to prove for longer so that the flavour develops fully. Italian breads also tend to have a crustier exterior. Look out

for Pugliese and ciabatta breads. Foccacia, a soft-crusted bread, is also popular and can be flavoured with herbs, sun-dried tomatoes or garlic.

Seafood

Italy has a large coastline relative to its size and, as a result, seafood is a very popular choice. A huge variety of fish and shellfish are available, and large meals such as those served at weddings or other special celebrations will always include a fish course.

Meat, Poultry and Game

Italians are amongst the world's greatest meat eaters. Most meals will be based on meat of some kind. Popular choices include beef, chicken, pork and lamb but duck, guinea fowl, pheasant, pigeon, rabbit, veal and many kinds of offal are also used.

How to Make Pasta

Home-made pasta has a light, almost silky texture. It is easy to make and little equipment is needed; just a rolling pin and a sharp knife, although if you make pasta regularly it is worth investing in a pasta machine.

Making Basic Egg Pasta Dough

Ingredients
225 g/8 oz type 001 pasta flour, plus extra for dusting
1 tsp salt
2 eggs, plus 1 egg yolk
1 tbsp olive oil
1–3 tsp cold water

1 Sift the flour and salt into a mound on a clean work surface and make a well in the middle, keeping the sides quite high, so that the egg mixture will not trickle out when added.
2 Beat together the eggs, yolk, oil and 1 teaspoon of water. Add to the well, then gradually work in the flour, adding extra water if needed, to make a soft but not sticky dough.
3 Knead on a lightly floured surface for 5 minutes, or until the dough is smooth and elastic. Wrap in clingfilm and leave to rest for 20 minutes at room temperature.

Using a Food Processor

Sift the flour and salt into a metal-bladed food processor. Add the eggs, yolk, oil and water and pulse-blend until the ingredients are mixed and until the dough begins to come together, adding the extra water if needed. Knead for 1–2 minutes, then wrap and rest as before.

Rolling Pasta by Hand

1 Unwrap the pasta dough and cut in half. Work with just half at a time and keep the other half wrapped in clingfilm.
2 Place the dough on a large, clean work surface lightly dusted with flour, then flatten with your hand and start to roll out. Always roll away from you, starting from the centre and giving the dough a quarter turn after each rolling. Sprinkle a little more flour over the dough if it starts to get sticky.
3 Continue rolling and turning until the dough is as thin as possible; ideally about 3 mm/⅛ inch. Make sure that you roll it evenly, or some shapes will cook faster than others.

Rolling Pasta by Machine

A machine makes smoother, thinner, more-even pasta than that made by hand-rolling. Most pasta machines work in the same way but you should refer to the manufacturers' instructions before using.

1 Clamp the machine securely and attach the handle. Set the rollers at their widest setting and sprinkle lightly with flour. Cut the pasta into four pieces. Wrap 3 in clingfilm and reserve.

2 Flatten the unwrapped pasta dough slightly, then feed it through the rollers. Fold the strip of dough in 3, rotate and feed through the rollers a second time. Continue to roll the pasta this way, narrowing the roller setting by one notch every second time and flouring the rollers if the pasta starts to get sticky. Only fold the dough the first time it goes through each roller width. The dough will get longer and thinner with every rolling – if it gets too difficult to handle, cut the strip in half and work with 1 piece at a time.

3 If making spaghetti or noodles such as tagliatelle, the second last setting is generally used. For pasta shapes and filled pastas, the dough should be rolled to the finest setting.

4 Fresh pasta should be dried slightly before cutting. Either drape over a narrow wooden pole for 5 minutes or place on a clean tea towel sprinkled with a little flour for 10 minutes.

You can also buy electric machines that carry out the whole pasta-making process. They can make over 900 g/2 lb of pasta at a time, but are expensive to buy and take up a lot of space.

Shaping Up

When cutting and shaping freshly made pasta, have 2 or 3 lightly floured tea-towels ready. Arrange the pasta in a single layer, spaced slightly apart. When dry, you can freeze them successfully for up to 6 weeks, by layering in suitable containers between sheets of baking parchment. Spread them out on baking parchment for about 20 minutes, or slightly longer if stuffed, before cooking.

Lasagne This is one of the easiest to make. Simply trim the pasta sheets until neat and cut into lengths the same size as your lasagne dish. Spread the cut sheets on tea towels sprinkled with flour.

Macaroni This is the generic name for hollow pasta. Cut the rolled-out pasta dough into squares, then wrap each around a chopstick, thick skewer or similar, starting from one of the corners. Slip the pasta off, curve slightly if liked and leave to dry for at least 15 minutes.

Noodles If using a pasta machine, use the cutter attachment to produce tagliatelle or fettucine, or use a narrower one for tagliarini or spaghetti. To make by hand, sprinkle the rolled-out pasta with flour, then roll up like a Swiss roll and cut into thin slices. The thickness of these depends on the noodles required. For linguine, cut into 5 mm/¼ inch slices and for tagliatelle cut into 8 mm/⅓ inch slices. Unravel them immediately after cutting. To make thicker ribbon pasta such as pappardelle, use a serrated pastry wheel to cut into wide strips. Leave over a wooden pole for up to 5 minutes to dry out.

Soups & Starters

White Bean Soup with Parmesan Croûtons

SERVES 4

3 thick slices of white bread, cut into 1 cm/½ inch cubes
3 tbsp groundnut oil
2 tbsp Parmesan cheese, finely grated
1 tbsp light olive oil
1 large onion, peeled and finely chopped

50 g/2 oz unsmoked bacon lardons (or thick slices of bacon, diced)
1 tbsp fresh thyme leaves
2 x 400 g cannellini beans, drained
900 ml/1½ pints chicken stock

salt and freshly ground black pepper
1 tbsp prepared pesto sauce
50 g/2 oz piece of pepperoni sausage, diced
1 tbsp fresh lemon juice
1 tbsp fresh basil, roughly shredded

Preheat oven to 200°C/400°F/Gas Mark 6. Place the cubes of bread in a bowl and pour over the groundnut oil. Stir to coat the bread, then sprinkle over the Parmesan cheese. Place on a lightly oiled baking tray and bake in the preheated oven for 10 minutes, or until crisp and golden.

Heat the olive oil in a large saucepan and cook the onion for 4–5 minutes until softened. Add the bacon and thyme and cook for a further 3 minutes. Stir in the beans, stock and black pepper and simmer gently for 5 minutes.

Place half the bean mixture and liquid into a food processor and blend until smooth.

Return the purée to the saucepan. Stir in the pesto sauce, pepperoni sausage and lemon juice and season to taste with salt and pepper.

Return the soup to the heat and cook for a further 2–3 minutes, or until piping hot. Place some of the beans in each serving bowl and add a ladleful of soup. Garnish with shredded basil and serve immediately with the croûtons scattered over the top.

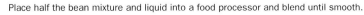

Try this: FOR AN ALTERNATIVE: 22   FOR A MORE SUBSTANTIAL OPTION: 254

Rich Tomato Soup with Roasted Red Peppers

SERVES 4

2 tsp light olive oil
700 g/1½ lb red peppers,
   halved and deseeded
450 g/1 lb ripe plum
   tomatoes, halved

2 onions, unpeeled and
   quartered
4 garlic cloves, unpeeled
600 ml/1 pint chicken stock
salt and freshly ground

black pepper
4 tbsp soured cream
1 tbsp freshly shredded basil

Preheat oven to 200°C/400°F/Gas Mark 6. Lightly oil a roasting tin with 1 teaspoon of the olive oil. Place the peppers and tomatoes cut side down in the roasting tin with the onion quarters and the garlic cloves. Spoon over the remaining oil.

Bake in the preheated oven for 30 minutes, or until the skins on the peppers have started to blacken and blister. Allow the vegetables to cool for about 10 minutes, then remove the skins, stalks and seeds from the peppers. Peel away the skins from the tomatoes and onions and squeeze out the garlic.

Place the cooked vegetables into a blender or food processor and blend until smooth. Add the stock and blend again to form a smooth purée. Pour the puréed soup through a sieve, if a smooth soup is preferred, then pour into a saucepan. Bring to the boil, simmer gently for 2–3 minutes, and season to taste with salt and pepper. Serve hot with a swirl of soured cream and a sprinkling of shredded basil on the top.

Try this: FOR AN ALTERNATIVE: 56   FOR A MORE SUBSTANTIAL OPTION: 250

Classic Minestrone

SERVES 6-8

25 g/1 oz butter
3 tbsp olive oil
3 rashers streaky bacon
1 large onion, peeled
1 garlic clove, peeled
1 celery stick, trimmed
2 carrots, peeled

400 g can chopped tomatoes
1.1 litre/2 pints chicken stock
175 g/6 oz green cabbage,
finely shredded
50 g/2 oz French beans,
trimmed and halved
3 tbsp frozen petits pois

50 g/2 oz spaghetti, broken
into short pieces
salt and freshly ground
black pepper
Parmesan cheese shavings,
to garnish
crusty bread, to serve

Heat the butter and olive oil together in a large saucepan. Chop the bacon and add to the saucepan. Cook for 3–4 minutes, then remove with a slotted spoon and reserve.

Finely chop the onion, garlic, celery and carrots and add to the saucepan, one ingredient at a time, stirring well after each addition. Cover and cook gently for 8–10 minutes, until the vegetables are softened.

Add the chopped tomatoes, with their juice and the stock, bring to the boil then cover the saucepan with a lid, reduce the heat and simmer gently for about 20 minutes.

Stir in the cabbage, beans, peas and spaghetti pieces. Cover and simmer for a further 20 minutes, or until all the ingredients are tender. Season to taste with salt and pepper.

Return the cooked bacon to the saucepan and bring the soup to the boil. Serve the soup immediately with Parmesan cheese shavings sprinkled on the top and plenty of crusty bread to accompany it.

Try this: FOR AN ALTERNATIVE: 20 FOR A MORE SUBSTANTIAL OPTION: 266

Cream of Pumpkin Soup

SERVES 4

900 g/2 lb pumpkin flesh
   (after peeling and
   discarding the seeds)
4 tbsp olive oil
1 large onion, peeled
1 leek, trimmed

1 carrot, peeled
2 celery sticks
4 garlic cloves, peeled and
   crushed
1.7 litres/3 pints water
salt and freshly ground

   black pepper
¼ tsp freshly grated nutmeg
150 ml/¼ pint single cream
¼ tsp cayenne pepper
warm herby bread, to serve

Cut the skinned and de-seeded pumpkin flesh into 2.5 cm/1 inch cubes. Heat the olive oil in a large saucepan and cook the pumpkin for 2–3 minutes, coating it completely with oil. Chop the onion and leek finely and cut the carrot and celery into small dice.

Add the vegetables to the saucepan with the garlic and cook, stirring for 5 minutes, or until they have begun to soften. Cover the vegetables with the water and bring to the boil. Season with plenty of salt and pepper and the nutmeg, cover and simmer for 15–20 minutes, or until all of the vegetables are tender.

When the vegetables are tender, remove from the heat, cool slightly then pour into a food processor or blender. Liquidise to form a smooth purée then pass through a sieve into a clean saucepan.

Adjust the seasoning to taste and add all but 2 tablespoons of the cream and enough water to obtain the correct consistency. Bring the soup to boiling point, add the cayenne pepper and serve immediately swirled with cream and warm herby bread.

Try this: FOR AN ALTERNATIVE: 18   FOR A MORE SUBSTANTIAL OPTION: 256

Lettuce Soup

SERVES 4

2 iceberg lettuces, quartered
   with hard core removed
1 tbsp olive oil
50 g/2 oz butter
125 g/4 oz spring onions,
   trimmed and chopped

1 tbsp freshly chopped
   parsley
1 tbsp plain flour
600 ml/1 pint chicken stock
salt and freshly ground
   black pepper

150 ml/¼ pint single cream
¼ tsp cayenne pepper,
   to taste
thick slices of stale
   ciabatta bread
sprig of parsley, to garnish

Bring a large saucepan of water to the boil and blanch the lettuce leaves for 3 minutes. Drain and dry thoroughly on absorbent kitchen paper. Then shred with a sharp knife.

Heat the oil and butter in a clean saucepan and add the lettuce, spring onions and parsley and cook together for 3–4 minutes, or until very soft.

Stir in the flour and cook for 1 minute, then gradually pour in the stock, stirring throughout. Bring to the boil and season to taste with salt and pepper. Reduce the heat, cover and simmer gently for 10–15 minutes, or until soft.

Allow the soup to cool slightly, then either sieve or purée in a blender. Alternatively, leave the soup chunky. Stir in the cream, add more seasoning, to taste, if liked, then add the cayenne pepper.

Arrange the slices of ciabatta bread in a large soup dish or in individual bowls and pour the soup over the bread. Garnish with sprigs of parsley and serve immediately.

Try this: FOR AN ALTERNATIVE: 16   FOR A MORE SUBSTANTIAL OPTION: 258

Antipasti with Focaccia

SERVES 4

3 fresh figs, quartered
125 g/4 oz green beans,
    cooked and halved
1 small head of radicchio,
    rinsed and shredded
125 g/4 oz large prawns,
    peeled and cooked
125 can sardines, drained

25 g/1 oz pitted black olives
25 g/1 oz stuffed green olives
125 g/4 oz mozzarella, sliced
50 g/2 oz Italian salami
    sausage, thinly sliced
3 tbsp olive oil
275 g/10 oz strong white flour
pinch of sugar

3 tsp easy-blend
    quick-acting yeast or 15
    g/½ oz fresh yeast
175 g/6 oz fine semolina
1 tsp salt
300 ml/½ pint warm water
a little extra oil for brushing
1 tbsp coarse salt crystals

Preheat oven to 220°C/425°F/Gas Mark 7, 15 minutes before baking. Arrange the fresh fruit, vegetables, prawns, sardines, olives, cheese and meat on a large serving platter. Drizzle over 1 tablespoon of the olive oil, then cover and chill in the refrigerator while making the bread.

Sift the flour, sugar, semolina and salt into a large mixing bowl then sprinkle in the dried yeast. Make a well in the centre and add the remaining 2 tablespoons of olive oil. Add the warm water, a little at a time, and mix together until a smooth, pliable dough is formed. If using fresh yeast, cream the yeast with the sugar, then gradually beat in half the warm water. Leave in a warm place until frothy then proceed as for dried yeast.

Place on to a lightly floured board and knead until smooth and elastic. Place the dough in a lightly greased bowl, cover and leave in a warm place for 45 minutes.

Knead again and flatten the dough into a large, flat oval shape about 1 cm/½ inch thick. Place on a lightly oiled baking tray. Prick the surface with the end of a wooden spoon and brush with olive oil. Sprinkle on the coarse salt and bake in the preheated oven for 25 minutes, or until golden. Serve the bread with the prepared platter of food.

Try this: FOR AN ALTERNATIVE: 34 FOR A MORE SUBSTANTIAL OPTION: 278

Mozzarella Frittata
with Tomato & Basil Salad

SERVES 6

For the salad:
6 ripe but firm tomatoes
2 tbsp fresh basil leaves
2 tbsp olive oil
1 tbsp fresh lemon juice
1 tsp caster sugar

freshly ground black pepper

For the frittata:
7 medium eggs, beaten
salt
300 g/11 oz mozzarella

2 spring onions, trimmed
 and finely chopped
2 tbsp olive oil
warm crusty bread, to serve

To make the tomato and basil salad, slice the tomatoes very thinly, tear up the basil leaves and sprinkle over. Make the dressing by whisking the olive oil, lemon juice and sugar together well. Season with black pepper before drizzling the dressing over the salad.

To make the frittata, preheat the grill to a high heat, just before beginning to cook. Place the eggs in a large bowl with plenty of salt and whisk. Grate the mozzarella and stir into the egg with the finely chopped spring onions.

Heat the oil in a large, non-stick frying pan and pour in the egg mixture, stirring with a wooden spoon to spread the ingredients evenly over the pan.

Cook for 5–8 minutes, until the frittata is golden brown and firm on the underside. Place the whole pan under the preheated grill and cook for about 4–5 minutes, or until the top is golden brown. Slide the frittata on to a serving plate, cut into 6 large wedges and serve immediately with the tomato and basil salad and plenty of warm crusty bread.

Try this: FOR AN ALTERNATIVE: 44 FOR A MORE SUBSTANTIAL OPTION: 262

Fried Whitebait
with Rocket Salad

SERVES 4

450 g/1 lb whitebait, fresh
   or frozen
oil, for frying
85 g/3 oz plain flour
½ tsp of cayenne pepper
salt and freshly ground

black pepper

For the salad:
125 g/4 oz rocket leaves
125 g/4 oz cherry
   tomatoes, halved

75 g/3 oz cucumber, cut
   into dice
3 tbsp olive oil
1 tbsp fresh lemon juice
½ tsp Dijon mustard
½ tsp caster sugar

If the whitebait are frozen, thaw completely, then wipe dry with absorbent kitchen paper.

Start to heat the oil in a deep-fat fryer. Arrange the fish in a large, shallow dish and toss well in the flour, cayenne pepper and salt and pepper.

Deep fry the fish in batches for 2–3 minutes, or until crisp and golden. Keep the cooked fish warm while deep frying the remaining fish.

Meanwhile, to make the salad, arrange the rocket leaves, cherry tomatoes and cucumber on individual serving dishes. Whisk the olive oil and the remaining ingredients together and season lightly. Drizzle the dressing over the salad and serve with the whitebait.

Try this: FOR AN ALTERNATIVE: 40 FOR A MORE SUBSTANTIAL OPTION: 120

Bruschetta with Pecorino, Garlic & Tomatoes

SERVES 4

6 ripe but firm tomatoes
125 g/4 oz pecorino cheese,
   finely grated
1 tbsp oregano leaves
salt and freshly ground

black pepper
3 tbsp olive oil
3 garlic cloves, peeled
8 slices of flat Italian bread,
   such as focaccia

50 g/2 oz mozzarella
marinated black olives,
   to serve

Preheat grill and line the grill rack with tinfoil just before cooking. Make a small cross in the top of the tomatoes, then place in a small bowl and cover with boiling water. Leave to stand for 2 minutes, then drain and remove the skins. Cut into quarters, remove the seeds, and chop the flesh into small dice.

Mix the tomato flesh with the pecorino cheese and 2 teaspoons of the fresh oregano and season to taste with salt and pepper. Add 1 tablespoon of the olive oil and mix thoroughly.

Crush the garlic and spread evenly over the slices of bread. Heat 2 tablespoons of the olive oil in a large frying pan and sauté the bread slices until they are crisp and golden.

Place the fried bread on a lightly oiled baking tray and spoon on the tomato and cheese topping. Place a little mozzarella on top and place under the preheated grill for 3–4 minutes, until golden and bubbling. Garnish with the remaining oregano, then arrange the bruschettas on a serving plate and serve immediately with the olives.

Try this: FOR AN ALTERNATIVE: 28   FOR A MORE SUBSTANTIAL OPTION: 264

Italian Baked Tomatoes with Curly Endive & Radicchio

SERVES 4

1 tsp olive oil
4 beef tomatoes
salt
50 g/2 oz fresh white
  breadcrumbs
1 tbsp freshly
  snipped chives
1 tbsp freshly

chopped parsley
125 g/4 oz button
  mushrooms, finely
  chopped
salt and freshly ground
  black pepper
25 g/1 oz fresh Parmesan
cheese, grated

For the salad:
½ curly endive lettuce
½ small piece of radicchio
2 tbsp olive oil
1 tsp balsamic vinegar
salt and freshly ground
  black pepper

Preheat oven to 190°C/375°F/Gas Mark 5. Lightly oil a baking tray with the teaspoon of oil. Slice the tops off the tomatoes and remove all the tomato flesh and sieve into a large bowl. Sprinkle a little salt inside the tomato shells and then place them upside down on a plate while the filling is prepared.

Mix the sieved tomato with the breadcrumbs, fresh herbs and mushrooms and season well with salt and pepper. Place the tomato shells on the prepared baking tray and fill with the tomato and mushroom mixture. Sprinkle the cheese on the top and bake in the preheated oven for 15–20 minutes, until golden brown.

Meanwhile, prepare the salad. Arrange the endive and radicchio on individual serving plates and mix the remaining ingredients together in a small bowl to make the dressing. Season to taste.

When the tomatoes are cooked, allow to rest for 5 minutes, then place on the prepared plates and drizzle over a little dressing. Serve warm.

Try this: FOR AN ALTERNATIVE: 218   FOR A MORE SUBSTANTIAL OPTION: 240

Spaghettini with Lemon Pesto & Cheese & Herb Bread

SERVES 4

1 small onion, peeled
   and grated
2 tsp freshly
   chopped oregano
1 tbsp freshly
   chopped parsley
75 g/3 oz butter
125 g/4 oz pecorino

cheese, grated
8 slices of Italian flat bread
275 g/10 oz dried spaghettini
4 tbsp olive oil
1 large bunch of basil,
   approximately 30 g/1 oz
75 g/3 oz pine nuts
1 garlic clove, peeled

and crushed
75 g/3 oz Parmesan
   cheese, grated
finely grated rind and juice
   of 2 lemons
salt and freshly ground
   black pepper
4 tsp butter

Preheat oven to 200°C/400°F/Gas Mark 6, 15 minutes before baking. Mix together the onion, oregano, parsley, butter and cheese. Spread the bread with the cheese mixture, place on a lightly oiled baking tray and cover with tinfoil. Bake in the preheated oven for 10–15 minutes, then keep warm.

Add the spaghettini with 1 tablespoon of olive oil to a large saucepan of fast-boiling, lightly salted water and cook for 3–4 minutes, or until 'al dente'. Drain, reserving 2 tablespoons of the cooking liquor.

Blend the basil, pine nuts, garlic, Parmesan cheese, lemon rind and juice and remaining olive oil in a food processor or blender until a purée is formed. Season to taste with salt and pepper, then place in a saucepan.

Heat the lemon pesto very gently until piping hot, then stir in the pasta together with the reserved cooking liquor. Add the butter and mix well together.

Add plenty of black pepper to the pasta and serve immediately with the warm cheese and herb bread.

Mussels with Creamy Garlic & Saffron Sauce

SERVES 4

700 g/1½ lb fresh live mussels
300 ml/½ pint good-quality dry white wine
1 tbsp olive oil
1 shallot, peeled and finely chopped
2 garlic cloves, peeled and crushed
1 tbsp freshly chopped oregano
2 saffron strands
150 ml/¼, pint single cream
salt and freshly ground black pepper
fresh crusty bread, to serve

Clean the mussels thoroughly in plenty of cold water and remove any beards and barnacles from the shells. Discard any mussels that are open or damaged. Place in a large bowl and cover with cold water and leave in the refrigerator until required, if prepared earlier.

Pour the wine into a large saucepan and bring to the boil. Tip the mussels into the pan, cover and cook, shaking the saucepan periodically for 6–8 minutes, or until the mussels have opened completely.

Discard any mussels with closed shells, then using a slotted spoon, carefully remove the remaining open mussels from the saucepan and keep them warm. Reserve the cooking liquor.

Heat the olive oil in a small frying pan and cook the shallot and garlic gently for 2–3 minutes, until softened. Add the reserved cooking liquid and chopped oregano and cook for a further 3–4 minutes. Stir in the saffron and the cream and heat through gently. Season to taste with salt and pepper. Place a few mussels in individual serving bowls and spoon over the saffron sauce. Serve immediately with plenty of fresh crusty bread.

Try this: FOR AN ALTERNATIVE: 114   FOR A MORE SUBSTANTIAL OPTION: 86

Hot Tiger Prawns with Parma Ham

SERVES 4

½ cucumber, peeled if
    preferred
4 ripe tomatoes
12 raw tiger prawns
6 tbsp olive oil

4 garlic cloves, peeled
    and crushed
4 tbsp freshly
    chopped parsley
salt and freshly ground

black pepper
6 slices of Parma ham,
    cut in half
4 slices flat Italian bread
4 tbsp dry white wine

Preheat oven to 180°C/350°F/Gas Mark 4. Slice the cucumber and tomatoes thinly, then arrange on 4 large plates and reserve. Peel the prawns, leaving the tail shell intact and remove the thin black vein running down the back.

Whisk together 4 tablespoons of the olive oil, garlic and chopped parsley in a small bowl and season to taste with plenty of salt and pepper. Add the prawns to the mixture and stir until they are well coated. Remove the prawns, then wrap each one in a piece of Parma ham and secure with a cocktail stick.

Place the prepared prawns on a lightly oiled baking sheet or dish with the slices of bread and cook in the preheated oven for 5 minutes.

Remove the prawns from the oven and spoon the wine over the prawns and bread. Return to the oven and cook for a further 10 minutes until piping hot.

Carefully remove the cocktail sticks and arrange 3 prawn rolls on each slice of bread. Place on top of the sliced cucumber and tomatoes and serve immediately.

 Try this: FOR AN ALTERNATIVE: 84 FOR A MORE SUBSTANTIAL OPTION: 302

Mozzarella Parcels with Cranberry Relish

SERVES 6

125 g/4 oz mozzarella
8 slices of thin white bread
2 medium eggs, beaten
salt and freshly ground
　black pepper

300 ml/½ pint olive oil

For the relish:
125 g/4 oz cranberries
2 tbsp fresh orange juice

grated rind of 1 small
　orange
50 g/2 oz soft light
　brown sugar
1 tbsp port

Slice the mozzarella thinly, remove the crusts from the bread and make sandwiches with the bread and cheese. Cut into 5 cm/2 inch squares and squash them quite flat. Season the eggs with salt and pepper, then soak the bread in the seasoned egg for 1 minute on each side until well coated.

Heat the oil to 190°C/375°F and deep-fry the bread squares for 1–2 minutes, or until they are crisp and golden brown. Drain on absorbent kitchen paper and keep warm while the cranberry relish is prepared.

Place the cranberries, orange juice, rind, sugar and port into a small saucepan and add 5 tablespoons of water. Bring to the boil, then simmer for 10 minutes, or until the cranberries have 'popped'. Sweeten with a little more sugar if necessary.

Arrange the mozzarella parcels on individual serving plates. Serve with a little of the relish.

Try this: FOR AN ALTERNATIVE: 52　FOR A MORE SUBSTANTIAL OPTION: 288

Fresh Tagliatelle with Courgettes

SERVES 4-6

225 g /8 oz strong plain bread flour or type 00 pasta flour, plus extra for rolling
1 tsp salt
2 medium eggs
1 medium egg yolk

3 tbsp extra virgin olive oil
2 small courgettes, halved lengthwise and thinly sliced
2 garlic cloves, peeled and thinly sliced
large pinch chilli flakes

zest of ½ lemon
1 tbsp freshly shredded basil
salt and freshly ground black pepper
freshly grated Parmesan cheese, to serve

Sift the flour and salt into a large bowl, make a well in the centre and add the eggs and yolk, 1 tablespoon of oil and 1 teaspoon of water. Gradually mix to form a soft but not sticky dough, adding a little more flour or water as necessary. Turn out on to a lightly floured surface and knead for 5 minutes, or until smooth and elastic. Wrap in clingfilm and leave to rest at room temperature for about 30 minutes. Divide the dough into 8 pieces. Feed a piece of dough through a pasta machine. Gradually decrease the settings on the rollers, feeding the pasta through each time, until the sheet is very long and thin. If the pasta seems sticky, dust the work surface and both sides of the pasta generously with flour. Cut in half crosswise and hang over a clean pole. Repeat with the remaining dough. Leave to dry for about 5 minutes. Feed each sheet through the tagliatelle cutter, hanging the cut pasta over the pole. Leave to dry for a further 5 minutes. Wind a handful of pasta strands into nests and leave on a floured tea towel. Repeat with the remaining dough and leave to dry for 5 minutes.

Cook the pasta in plenty of salted boiling water for 2–3 minutes, or until 'al dente'. Meanwhile, heat the remaining oil in a large frying pan and add the courgettes, garlic, chilli and lemon zest. Cook over a medium heat for 3–4 minutes, or until the courgettes are lightly golden and tender. Drain the pasta thoroughly, reserving 2 tablespoons of the cooking water. Add the pasta to the courgettes with the basil and seasoning. Mix well, adding the reserved cooking water. Serve with the Parmesan cheese.

Try this: FOR AN ALTERNATIVE: 66   FOR A MORE SUBSTANTIAL OPTION: 280

Beetroot Ravioli
with Dill Cream Sauce

SERVES 4-6

fresh pasta (see Fresh
  Tagliatelle with
  Courgettes, page 50)
1 tbsp olive oil
1 small onion, peeled and
  finely chopped
½ tsp caraway seeds
175 g/6 oz cooked

beetroot, chopped
175 g/6 oz ricotta cheese
25 g/1 oz fresh white
  breadcrumbs
1 medium egg yolk
2 tbsp grated Parmesan
  cheese
salt and freshly ground

black pepper
4 tbsp walnut oil
4 tbsp freshly chopped dill
1 tbsp green peppercorns,
  drained and roughly
  chopped
6 tbsp crème fraîche

Make the pasta dough according to the recipe on page 140. Wrap in clingfilm and leave to rest for 30 minutes.

Heat the olive oil in a large frying pan, add the onion and caraway seeds and cook over a medium heat for 5 minutes, or until the onion is softened and lightly golden. Stir in the beetroot and cook for 5 minutes. Blend the beetroot mixture in a food processor until smooth, then allow to cool. Stir in the ricotta cheese, breadcrumbs, egg yolk and Parmesan cheese. Season the filling to taste with salt and pepper and reserve.

Divide the pasta dough into 8 pieces. Roll out as for tagliatelle, but do not cut the sheets in half. Lay 1 sheet on a floured surface and place 5 heaped teaspoons of the filling 2.5 cm/1 inch apart. Dampen around the heaps of filling and lay a second sheet of pasta over the top. Press around the heaps to seal. Cut into squares using a pastry wheel or sharp knife. Put the filled pasta shapes on to a floured tea towel.

Bring a pan of lightly salted water to a rolling boil. Drop in the ravioli, return to the boil and cook for 3–4 minutes, or until 'al dente'. Meanwhile, heat the walnut oil in a small pan then add the chopped dill and green peppercorns. Remove from the heat, stir in the crème fraîche and season well. Drain the cooked pasta and toss with the sauce. Serve immediately in warmed dishes.

Try this: FOR AN ALTERNATIVE: 44 FOR A MORE SUBSTANTIAL OPTION: 242

Spinach & Ricotta Gnocchi with Butter & Parmesan

SERVES 2-4

125 g/4 oz frozen leaf
  spinach, thawed
225 g/8 oz ricotta cheese
2 small eggs, lightly beaten
50 g/2 oz freshly grated

Parmesan cheese
salt and freshly ground
  black pepper
2 tbsp freshly chopped basil
50 g/2 oz plain flour

50 g/2 oz unsalted butter
2 garlic cloves, peeled
  and crushed
Parmesan cheese shavings,
  to serve

Squeeze the excess moisture from the spinach and chop finely. Blend in a food processor with the ricotta cheese, eggs, Parmesan cheese, seasoning and 1 tablespoon of the basil until smooth. Scrape into a bowl then add sufficient flour to form a soft, slightly sticky dough.

Bring a large pan of salted water to a rolling boil. Transfer the spinach mixture to a piping bag fitted with a large plain nozzle. As soon as the water is boiling, pipe 10–12 short lengths of the mixture into the water, using a sharp knife to cut the gnocchi as you go.

Bring the water back to the boil and cook the gnocchi for 3–4 minutes, or until they begin to rise to the surface. Remove with a slotted spoon, drain on absorbent kitchen paper and transfer to a warmed serving dish. Cook the gnocchi in batches if necessary.

Melt the butter in a small frying pan and when foaming add the garlic and remaining basil. Remove from the heat and immediately pour over the cooked gnocchi. Season well with salt and pepper and serve immediately with extra grated Parmesan cheese.

Tagliatelle with Brown Butter, Asparagus & Parmesan

SERVES 6

fresh pasta (see Fresh Tagliatelle with Courgettes, page 50) or 450 g/1 lb dried tagliatelle, such as the white and green variety
350 g/12 oz asparagus, trimmed and cut into

short lengths
75 g/3 oz unsalted butter
1 garlic clove, peeled and sliced
25 g/1 oz flaked hazelnuts or whole hazelnuts, roughly chopped
1 tbsp freshly

chopped parsley
1 tbsp freshly snipped chives
salt and freshly ground black pepper
50 g/2 oz freshly grated Parmesan cheese, to serve

If using fresh pasta, prepare the dough according to the recipe on page 16. Cut into tagliatelle, wind into nests and reserve on a floured tea towel until ready to cook.

Bring a pan of lightly salted water to the boil. Add the asparagus and cook for 1 minute. Drain immediately, refresh under cold running water and drain again. Pat dry and reserve.

Melt the butter in a large frying pan, then add the garlic and hazelnuts and cook over a medium heat until the butter turns golden. Immediately remove from the heat and add the parsley, chives and asparagus. Leave for 2–3 minutes, until the asparagus is heated through.

Meanwhile, bring a large pan of lightly salted water to a rolling boil, then add the pasta nests. Cook until 'al dente': 2–3 minutes for fresh pasta and according to the packet instructions for dried pasta. Drain the pasta thoroughly and return to the pan. Add the asparagus mixture and toss together. Season to taste with salt and pepper and tip into a warmed serving dish. Serve immediately with grated Parmesan cheese.

Try this: FOR AN ALTERNATIVE: 58 FOR A MORE SUBSTANTIAL OPTION: 204

Spaghetti with Fresh Tomatoes, Chilli & Potatoes

SERVES 6

2 medium potatoes,
 unpeeled
3 garlic cloves, peeled
 and crushed
1 small bunch basil,
 roughly chopped

6 tbsp olive oil
4 large ripe plum tomatoes,
 skinned, seeded and
 chopped
1 small red chilli, deseeded
 and finely chopped

salt and freshly ground
 black pepper
450 g/1 lb spaghetti
4 tbsp freshly grated
 Parmesan cheese, to
 serve (optional)

Preheat the grill to high 5 minutes before using. Cook the potatoes in plenty of boiling water until tender but firm. Allow to cool, then peel and cut into cubes.

Blend the garlic, basil and 4 tablespoons of the olive oil in a blender or food processor until the basil is finely chopped, then reserve.

Place the tomatoes, basil and oil mixture in a small bowl, add the chilli and season with salt and pepper to taste. Mix together and reserve the sauce.

Bring a large pan of salted water to a rolling boil, add the spaghetti and cook according to the packet instructions, or until 'al dente'.

Meanwhile, toss the potato cubes with the remaining olive oil and transfer to a baking sheet. Place the potatoes under the preheated grill until they are crisp and golden, turning once or twice, then drain on absorbent kitchen paper.

Drain the pasta thoroughly and transfer to a warmed shallow serving bowl. Add the tomato sauce and the hot potatoes. Toss well and adjust the seasoning to taste. Serve immediately with the grated Parmesan cheese, if using.

Try this: FOR AN ALTERNATIVE: 56 FOR A MORE SUBSTANTIAL OPTION: 112

Fusilli with Spicy Tomato & Chorizo Sauce with Roasted Peppers

SERVES 6

4 tbsp olive oil
1 red pepper, deseeded
   and quartered
1 yellow pepper, deseeded
   and quartered
175 g/6 oz chorizo (outer
   skin removed),

roughly chopped
2 garlic cloves, peeled and
   finely chopped
large pinch chilli flakes
700 g/1½ lb ripe tomatoes,
   skinned and roughly
   chopped

salt and freshly ground
   black pepper
450 g/1 lb fusilli
basil leaves, to garnish
freshly grated Parmesan
   cheese, to serve

Preheat the grill to high. Brush the pepper quarters with 1 tablespoon of the olive oil, then cook under the preheated grill, turning once, for 8–10 minutes, or until the skins have blackened and the flesh is tender. Place the peppers in a plastic bag until cool enough to handle. When cooled, peel the peppers, slice very thinly and reserve.

Heat the remaining oil in a frying pan and add the chorizo. Cook over a medium heat for 3–4 minutes, or until starting to brown. Add the garlic and chilli flakes and cook for a further 2–3 minutes.

Add the tomatoes, season lightly with salt and pepper then cook gently for about 5 minutes, or until the tomatoes have broken down. Lower the heat and cook for a further 10–15 minutes, or until the sauce has thickened. Add the peppers and heat gently for 1-2 minutes. Adjust the seasoning to taste.

Meanwhile, bring a large pan of lightly salted water to a rolling boil. Add the fusilli and cook according to the packet instructions, or until 'al dente'. Drain thoroughly and transfer to a warmed serving dish. Pour over the sauce, sprinkle with basil and serve with Parmesan cheese.

Try this: FOR AN ALTERNATIVE: 62 FOR A MORE SUBSTANTIAL OPTION: 154

Pasta with Walnut Sauce

SERVES 4

50 g/2 oz walnuts, toasted
3 spring onions, trimmed
    and chopped
2 garlic cloves, peeled
    and sliced

1 tbsp freshly chopped
    parsley or basil
5 tbsp extra virgin olive oil
salt and freshly ground
    black pepper

450 g/1 lb broccoli, cut
    into florets
350 g/12 oz pasta shapes
1 red chilli, deseeded and
    finely chopped

Place the toasted walnuts in a blender or food processor with the chopped spring onions, one of the garlic cloves and parsley or basil. Blend to a fairly smooth paste, then gradually add 3 tablespoons of the olive oil, until it is well mixed into the paste. Season the walnut paste to taste with salt and pepper and reserve.

Bring a large pan of lightly salted water to a rolling boil. Add the broccoli, return to the boil and cook for 2 minutes. Remove the broccoli, using a slotted draining spoon and refresh under cold running water. Drain again and pat dry on absorbent kitchen paper.

Bring the water back to a rolling boil. Add the pasta and cook according to the packet instructions, or until 'al dente'.

Meanwhile, heat the remaining oil in a frying pan. Add the remaining garlic and chilli. Cook gently for 2 minutes, or until softened. Add the broccoli and walnut paste. Cook for a further 3–4 minutes, or until heated through.

Drain the pasta thoroughly and transfer to a large warmed serving bowl. Pour over the walnut and broccoli sauce. Toss together, adjust the seasoning and serve immediately.

Try this: FOR AN ALTERNATIVE: 66   FOR A MORE SUBSTANTIAL OPTION: 284

Gnocchetti with Broccoli & Bacon Sauce

SERVES 6

450 g/1 lb broccoli florets
4 tbsp olive oil
50 g/2 oz pancetta or
  smoked bacon,
  finely chopped
1 small onion, peeled and

finely chopped
3 garlic cloves, peeled
  and sliced
200 ml/7 fl oz milk
450 g/1 lb gnocchetti (little
  elongated ribbed shells)

50 g/2 oz freshly grated
  Parmesan cheese, plus
  extra to serve
salt and freshly ground
  black pepper

Bring a large pan of salted water to the boil. Add the broccoli florets and cook for about 8–10 minutes, or until very soft. Drain thoroughly, allow to cool slightly then chop finely and reserve.

Heat the olive oil in a heavy-based pan, add the pancetta or bacon and cook over a medium heat for 5 minutes, or until golden and crisp. Add the onion and cook for a further 5 minutes, or until soft and lightly golden. Add the garlic and cook for 1 minute.

Transfer the chopped broccoli to the bacon or pancetta mixture and pour in the milk. Bring slowly to the boil and simmer rapidly for about 15 minutes, or until reduced to a creamy texture.

Meanwhile, bring a large pan of lightly salted water to a rolling boil. Add the pasta and cook according to the packet instructions, or until 'al dente'.

Drain the pasta thoroughly, reserving a little of the cooking water. Add the pasta and the Parmesan cheese to the broccoli mixture. Toss, adding enough of the reserved cooking water to make a creamy sauce. Season to taste with salt and pepper. Serve immediately with extra Parmesan cheese.

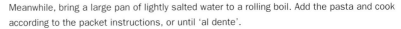

Try this: FOR AN ALTERNATIVE: 50 FOR A MORE SUBSTANTIAL OPTION: 270

Penne with Artichokes, Bacon & Mushrooms

SERVES 6

2 tbsp olive oil
75 g/3 oz smoked bacon or pancetta, chopped
1 small onion, peeled and finely sliced
125 g/4 oz chestnut mushrooms, wiped and sliced
2 garlic cloves, peeled and finely chopped
400 g/14 oz can artichoke hearts, drained and halved or quartered if large
100 ml/3½ fl oz dry white wine
100 ml/3½ fl oz chicken stock
3 tbsp double cream
50 g/2 oz freshly grated Parmesan cheese, plus extra to serve
salt and freshly ground black pepper
450 g/1 lb penne
shredded basil leaves, to garnish

Heat the olive oil in a frying pan and add the pancetta or bacon and the onion. Cook over a medium heat for 8–10 minutes, or until the bacon is crisp and the onion is just golden. Add the mushrooms and garlic and cook for a further 5 minutes, or until softened.

Add the artichoke hearts to the mushroom mixture and cook for 3–4 minutes. Pour in the wine, bring to the boil then simmer rapidly until the liquid is reduced and syrupy.

Pour in the chicken stock, bring to the boil then simmer rapidly for about 5 minutes, or until slightly reduced. Reduce the heat slightly, then slowly stir in the double cream and Parmesan cheese. Season the sauce to taste with salt and pepper.

Meanwhile, bring a large pan of lightly salted water to a rolling boil. Add the pasta and cook according to the packet instructions, or until 'al dente'.

Drain the pasta thoroughly and transfer to a large warmed serving dish. Pour over the sauce and toss together. Garnish with shredded basil and serve with extra Parmesan cheese.

Try this: FOR AN ALTERNATIVE: 64 FOR A MORE SUBSTANTIAL OPTION: 130

Fettuccine with Wild Mushrooms & Prosciutto

SERVES 6

15 g/½ oz dried porcini mushrooms
150 ml/¼ pint hot chicken stock
2 tbsp olive oil
1 small onion, peeled and finely chopped
2 garlic cloves, peeled and finely chopped
4 slices prosciutto, chopped or torn
225 g/8 oz mixed wild or cultivated mushrooms, wiped and sliced if necessary
450 g/1 lb fettuccine
3 tbsp crème fraîche
2 tbsp freshly chopped parsley
salt and freshly ground black pepper
freshly grated Parmesan cheese, to serve (optional)

Place the dried mushrooms in a small bowl and pour over the hot chicken stock. Leave to soak for 15–20 minutes, or until the mushrooms have softened.

Meanwhile, heat the olive oil in a large frying pan. Add the onion and cook for 5 minutes over a medium heat, or until softened. Add the garlic and cook for 1 minute, then add the prosciutto and cook for a further minute.

Drain the dried mushrooms, reserving the soaking liquid. Roughly chop and add to the frying pan together with the fresh mushrooms. Cook over a high heat for 5 minutes, stirring often, or until softened. Strain the mushroom soaking liquid into the pan.

Meanwhile, bring a large pan of lightly salted water to a rolling boil. Add the pasta and cook according to the packet instructions, or until 'al dente'.

Stir the crème fraîche and chopped parsley into the mushroom mixture and heat through gently. Season to taste with salt and pepper. Drain the pasta well, transfer to a large warmed serving dish and pour over the sauce. Serve immediately with grated Parmesan cheese.

Try this: FOR AN ALTERNATIVE: 56 FOR A MORE SUBSTANTIAL OPTION: 190

Tagliarini with Broad Beans, Saffron & Crème Fraîche

SERVES 2-3

225 g/8 oz fresh young broad beans in pods or 100 g/3½ oz frozen broad beans, thawed
1 tbsp olive oil
1 garlic clove, peeled

and chopped
small handful basil leaves, shredded
200 ml/7 fl oz crème fraîche
large pinch saffron strands
350 g/12 oz tagliarini

salt and freshly ground black pepper
1 tbsp freshly snipped chives
freshly grated Parmesan cheese, to serve

If using fresh broad beans, bring a pan of lightly salted water to the boil. Pod the beans and drop them into the boiling water for 1 minute. Drain and refresh under cold water. Drain again. Remove the outer skin of the beans and discard. If using thawed frozen broad beans, remove and discard the skins. Reserve the peeled beans.

Heat the olive oil in a saucepan. Add the peeled broad beans and the garlic and cook gently for 2–3 minutes. Stir in the basil, the crème fraîche and the pinch of saffron strands and simmer for 1 minute.

Meanwhile, bring a large pan of lightly salted water to a rolling boil. Add the pasta and cook according to the packet instructions, or until 'al dente'. Drain the pasta well and add to the sauce. Toss together and season to taste with salt and pepper.

Transfer the pasta and sauce to a warmed serving dish. Sprinkle with snipped chives and serve immediately with Parmesan cheese.

Try this: FOR AN ALTERNATIVE: 46   FOR A MORE SUBSTANTIAL OPTION: 82

Linguine with Fennel, Crab & Chervil

SERVES 6

450g/1 lb linguine
25 g/1 oz butter
2 carrots, peeled and
  finely diced
2 shallots, peeled and
  finely diced
2 celery sticks, trimmed

and finely diced
1 bulb fennel, trimmed
  and finely diced
6 spring onions, trimmed
  and finely chopped
300 ml/½ pint double cream
3 tbsp freshly chopped

chervil
1 large cooked crab
plus extra for garnish
salt and freshly ground
  pepper
juice of ½ lemon, or to taste
sprig of dill, to garnish

Bring a large pan of lightly salted water to a rolling boil. Add the pasta and cook according to the packet instructions, or until 'al dente'.

Meanwhile, heat the butter in a large saucepan. Add the carrots, shallots, celery, fennel and three-quarters of the chopped spring onions. Cook the vegetables gently for 8–10 minutes, or until tender, stirring frequently and ensuring that they do not brown.

Add the double cream and chopped chervil to the vegetable mixture. Scrape the crab meat over the sauce, then stir to mix the sauce ingredients.

Season the sauce to taste with salt and pepper and stir in the lemon juice. Drain the pasta thoroughly and transfer to a large warmed serving dish. Pour over the sauce and toss. Garnish with extra chervil, the remaining spring onions and a sprig of dill. Serve immediately.

Try this: FOR AN ALTERNATIVE: 32   FOR A MORE SUBSTANTIAL OPTION: 96

Fish & Shellfish

Pea & Prawn Risotto

SERVES 6

450 g/1 lb whole raw prawns
125 g/4 oz butter
1 red onion, peeled
  and chopped
4 garlic cloves, peeled and

finely chopped
225 g/8 oz Arborio rice
150 ml/¼ pint dry white wine
1.1 litres/2 pints vegetable
  or fish stock

375 g/13 oz frozen peas
4 tbsp freshly chopped mint
salt and freshly ground
  black pepper

Peel the prawns and reserve the heads and shells. Remove the black vein from the back of each prawn, then wash and dry on absorbent kitchen paper. Melt half the butter in a large frying pan, add the prawns' heads and shells and fry, stirring occasionally for 3–4 minutes, or until golden. Strain the butter, discard the heads and shells and return the butter to the pan.

Add a further 25 g/1 oz of butter to the pan and fry the onion and garlic for 5 minutes until softened, but not coloured. Add the rice and stir the grains in the butter for 1 minute, until they are coated thoroughly. Add the white wine and boil rapidly until the wine is reduced by half.

Bring the stock to a gentle simmer, and add to the rice, a ladleful at a time. Stir constantly, adding the stock as it is absorbed, until the rice is creamy, but still has a bite in the centre.

Melt the remaining butter and stir-fry the prawns for 3–4 minutes. Stir into the rice, along with all the pan juices and the peas. Add the chopped mint and season to taste with salt and pepper. Cover the pan and leave the prawns to infuse for 5 minutes before serving.

Try this: FOR AN ALTERNATIVE: 96 FOR A LIGHT BITE: 42

Stuffed Squid with Romesco Sauce

SERVES 4

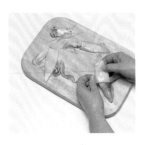

8 small squid, about
350 g/12 oz
5 tbsp olive oil
50 g/2 oz pancetta, diced
1 onion, peeled
and chopped
3 garlic cloves, peeled and
finely chopped
2 tsp freshly chopped thyme

50 g/2 oz sun-dried
tomatoes in oil drained,
and chopped
75 g/3 oz fresh white
breadcrumbs
2 tbsp freshly chopped basil
juice of ½ lime
salt and freshly ground
black pepper

2 vine-ripened tomatoes,
peeled and finely chopped
pinch of dried chilli flakes
1 tsp dried oregano
1 large red pepper, skinned
and chopped
assorted salad leaves,
to serve

Preheat oven to 230°C/450°F/Gas Mark 8, 15 minutes before cooking. Clean the squid if necessary, rinse lightly, pat dry with absorbent kitchen paper and finely chop the tentacles.

Heat 2 tablespoons of the olive oil in a large non-stick frying pan and fry the pancetta for 5 minutes, or until crisp. Remove the pancetta and reserve. Add the tentacles, onion, 2 garlic cloves, thyme and sun-dried tomatoes to the oil remaining in the pan and cook gently for 5 minutes, or until softened.

Remove the pan from the heat and stir in the diced pancetta. Blend in a food processor if a smoother stuffing is preferred, then stir in the breadcrumbs, basil and lime juice. Season to taste with salt and pepper and reserve. Spoon the stuffing into the cavity of the squid and secure the tops with cocktail sticks. Place the squid in a large roasting tin, and sprinkle over 2 tablespoons each of oil and water. Place in the preheated oven and cook for 20 minutes.

Heat the remaining oil in a saucepan and cook the remaining garlic for 3 minutes. Add the tomatoes, chilli flakes and oregano and simmer gently for 15 minutes. Stir in the red pepper. Cook gently for a further 5 minutes. Blend in a food processor to make a smooth sauce and season to taste. Pour the sauce over the squid and serve with assorted salad leaves.

Try this: FOR AN ALTERNATIVE: 112 FOR A LIGHT BITE: 68

Scallops & Monkfish Kebabs with Fennel Sauce

SERVES 4

700 g/1½ lb monkfish tail
8 large fresh scallops
2 tbsp olive oil
1 garlic clove, peeled
   and crushed
freshly ground black pepper

1 fennel bulb, trimmed and
   thinly sliced
assorted salad leaves, to serve

For the sauce:
2 tbsp fennel seeds

pinch of chilli flakes
4 tbsp olive oil
2 tsp lemon juice
salt and freshly ground
   black pepper

Place the monkfish on a chopping board and remove the skin and the bone that runs down the centre of the tail and discard. Lightly rinse and pat dry with absorbent kitchen paper. Cut the 2 fillets into 12 equal-sized pieces and place in a shallow bowl. Remove the scallops from their shells, if necessary, and clean thoroughly discarding the black vein. Rinse lightly and pat dry with absorbent kitchen paper. Put in the bowl with the fish.

Blend the 2 tablespoons of olive oil, the crushed garlic and a pinch of black pepper in a small bowl, then pour the mixture over the monkfish and scallops, making sure they are well coated. Cover lightly and leave to marinate in the refrigerator for at least 30 minutes, or longer if time permits. Spoon over the marinade occasionally.

Lightly crush the fennel seeds and chilli flakes in a pestle and mortar. Stir in the 4 tablespoons of olive oil and lemon juice and season to taste with salt and pepper. Cover and leave to infuse for 20 minutes.

Drain the monkfish and scallops, reserving the marinade and thread on to 4 skewers. Spray a griddle pan with a fine spray of oil, then heat until almost smoking and cook the kebabs for 5–6 minutes, turning halfway through and brushing with the marinade throughout. Brush the fennel slices with the fennel sauce and cook on the griddle for 1 minute on each side. Serve the fennel slices, topped with the kebabs and drizzled with the fennel sauce. Serve with salad leaves.

Try this: FOR AN ALTERNATIVE: 106 FOR A LIGHT BITE: 40

Sardines in Vine Leaves

SERVES 4

8–16 vine leaves in
    brine, drained
2 spring onions
6 tbsp olive oil
2 tbsp lime juice
2 tbsp freshly

chopped oregano
1 tsp mustard powder
salt and freshly ground
    black pepper
8 sardines, cleaned
8 bay leaves

8 sprigs of fresh dill
lime wedges, to garnish
sprigs of fresh dill, to
    garnish
olive salad, to serve
crusty bread, to serve

Preheat the grill and line the grill rack with tinfoil just before cooking. Cut 8 pieces of string about 25.5 cm/10 inches long, and leave to soak in cold water for about 10 minutes. Cover the vine leaves in almost boiling water. Leave for 20 minutes, then drain and rinse thoroughly. Pat the vine leaves dry with absorbent kitchen paper.

Trim the spring onions and finely chop, then place into a small bowl. With a balloon whisk beat in the olive oil, lime juice, oregano, mustard powder and season to taste with salt and pepper. Cover with clingfilm and leave in the refrigerator, until required. Stir the mixture before using.

Prepare the sardines, by making 2 slashes on both sides of each fish and brush with a little of the lime juice mixture. Place a bay leaf and a dill sprig inside each sardine cavity and wrap with 1–2 vine leaves, depending on size. Brush with the lime mixture and tie the vine leaves in place with string.

Grill the fish for 4–5 minutes on each side under a medium heat, brushing with a little more of the lime mixture if necessary. Leave the fish to rest, unwrap and discard the vine leaves. Garnish with lime wedges and sprigs of fresh dill and serve with the remaining lime mixture, olive salad and crusty bread.

Try this: FOR AN ALTERNATIVE: 120   FOR A LIGHT BITE: 32

Parmesan & Garlic Lobster

SERVES 2

1 large cooked lobster
25 g/1 oz unsalted butter
4 garlic cloves, peeled
    and crushed

1 tbsp plain flour
300 ml/½ pint milk
125 g/4 oz Parmesan
    cheese, grated

sea salt and freshly ground
    black pepper
assorted salad leaves,
    to serve

Preheat oven to 180°C/350°F/Gas Mark 4, 10 minutes before cooking. Halve the lobster and crack the claws. Remove the gills, green sac behind the head and the black vein running down the body. Place the 2 lobster halves in a shallow ovenproof dish.

Melt the butter in a small saucepan and gently cook the garlic for 3 minutes, until softened. Add the flour and stir over a medium heat for 1 minute. Draw the saucepan off the heat then gradually stir in the milk, stirring until the sauce thickens. Return to the heat and cook for 2 minutes, stirring throughout until smooth and thickened. Stir in half the cheese and continue to cook for 1 minute, then season to taste with salt and pepper.

Pour the cheese sauce over the lobster halves and sprinkle with the remaining Parmesan cheese. Bake in the preheated oven for 20 minutes, or until heated through and the cheese sauce is golden brown. Serve with assorted salad leaves.

Try this: FOR AN ALTERNATIVE: 92 FOR A LIGHT BITE: 42

Roasted Cod with Saffron Aïoli

SERVES 4

For the saffron aïoli:
2 garlic cloves, peeled
¼tsp saffron strands
sea salt, to taste
1 medium egg yolk
200 ml/7 fl oz extra-virgin
   olive oil
2 tbsp lemon juice

For the marinade:
2 tbsp olive oil
4 garlic cloves, peeled and
   finely chopped
1 red onion, peeled and
   finely chopped
1 tbsp freshly chopped
   rosemary

2 tbsp freshly chopped
   thyme
4–6 sprigs of fresh rosemary
1 lemon, sliced
4 x 175 g/6 oz thick cod
   fillets with skin
freshly cooked vegtables,
   to serve

Preheat oven to 180°C/350°F/Gas Mark 4, 10 minutes before cooking. Crush the garlic, saffron and a pinch of salt in a pestle and mortar to form a paste. Place in a blender with the egg yolk and blend for 30 seconds. With the motor running, slowly add the olive oil in a thin, steady stream until the mayonnaise is smooth and thick. Spoon into a small bowl and stir in the lemon juice. Cover and leave in the refrigerator until required.

Combine the olive oil, garlic, red onion, rosemary and thyme for the marinade and leave to infuse for about 10 minutes.

Place the sprigs of rosemary and slices of lemon in the bottom of a lightly oiled roasting tin. Add the cod, skinned -side up. Pour over the prepared marinade and leave to marinate in the refrigerator for 15–20 minutes. Bake in the preheated oven for 15–20 minutes, or until the cod is cooked and the flesh flakes easily with a fork. Leave the cod to rest for 1 minute before serving with the saffron aïoli and vegetables.

Try this: FOR AN ALTERNATIVE: 84 FOR A LIGHT BITE: 66

Roasted Monkfish with Parma Ham

SERVES 4

700 g/1½ lb monkfish tail
sea salt and freshly ground
    black pepper
4 bay leaves
4 slices fontina cheese,
    rind removed

8 slices Parma ham
225 g/8 oz angel hair pasta
50 g/2 oz butter
the zest and juice of 1 lemon
sprigs of fresh coriander,
    to garnish

chargrilled courgettes,
    to serve
chargrilled tomatoes,
    to serve

Preheat oven to 200°C/400°F/Gas Mark 6, 15 minutes before cooking. Discard any skin from the monkfish tail and cut away and discard the central bone. Cut the fish into 4 equal-sized pieces and season to taste with salt and pepper and lay a bay leaf on each fillet, along with a slice of cheese.

Wrap each fillet with 2 slices of the Parma ham, so that the fish is covered completely. Tuck the ends of the Parma ham in and secure with a cocktail stick.

Lightly oil a baking sheet and place in the preheated oven for a few minutes. Place the fish on the preheated baking sheet, then place in the oven and cook for 12–15 minutes.

Bring a large saucepan of lightly salted water to the boil, then slowly add the pasta and cook for 5 minutes until 'al dente', or according to packet directions. Drain, reserving 2 tablespoons of the pasta-cooking liquor. Return the pasta to the saucepan and add the reserved pasta liquor, butter, lemon zest and juice. Toss until the pasta is well coated and glistening.

Twirl the pasta into small nests on 4 warmed serving plates and top with the monkfish parcels. Garnish with sprigs of coriander and serve with chargrilled courgettes and tomatoes.

Try this: FOR AN ALTERNATIVE: 76   FOR A LIGHT BITE: 64

Mussels Arrabbiata

SERVES 4

1.8 kg/4 lb mussels
3–4 tbsp olive oil
1 large onion, peeled and sliced
4 garlic cloves, peeled and finely chopped

1 red chilli, deseeded and finely chopped
3 x 400 g cans chopped tomatoes
150 ml/¼ pint white wine
175 g/6 oz black olives,

pitted and halved
salt and freshly ground black pepper
2 tbsp freshly chopped parsley
warm crusty bread, to serve

Clean the mussels by scrubbing with a small, soft brush, removing the beard and any barnacles from the shells. Discard any mussels that are open or have damaged shells. Place in a large bowl and cover with cold water. Change the water frequently before cooking and leave in the refrigerator until required.

Heat the olive oil in a large saucepan and sweat the onion, garlic and chilli until soft, but not coloured. Add the tomatoes and bring to the boil, then simmer for 15 minutes.

Add the white wine to the tomato sauce, bring the sauce to the boil and add the mussels. Cover and carefully shake the pan. Cook the mussels for 5–7 minutes, or until the shells have opened.

Add the olives to the pan and cook uncovered for about 5 minutes to warm through. Season to taste with salt and pepper and sprinkle in the chopped parsley. Discard any mussels that have not opened and serve immediately with lots of warm crusty bread.

Tuna Cannelloni

SERVES 4

1 tbsp olive oil
6 spring onions, trimmed
   and finely sliced
1 sweet Mediterranean
   red pepper, deseeded and
   finely chopped
200 g can tuna in brine
250 g tub ricotta cheese

zest and juice of 1 lemon
1 tbsp freshly
   snipped chives
salt and freshly ground
   black pepper
8 dried cannelloni tubes
1 medium egg, beaten
125 g/4 oz cottage cheese

150 ml/¼ pint natural yogurt
pinch of freshly
   grated nutmeg
50 g/2 oz mozzarella
   cheese, grated
tossed green salad, to serve

Preheat oven to 180°C/375°F/Gas Mark 5, 10 minutes before cooking. Heat the olive oil in a frying pan and cook the spring onions and pepper until soft. Remove from the pan with a slotted draining spoon and place in large bowl.

Drain the tuna, then stir into the spring onions and pepper. Beat the ricotta cheese with the lemon zest and juice, and the snipped chives and season to taste with salt and pepper until soft and blended. Add to the tuna and mix together. If the mixture is still a little stiff, add a little extra lemon juice.

With a teaspoon, carefully spoon the mixture into the cannelloni tubes, then lay the filled tubes in a lightly oiled shallow ovenproof dish. Beat the egg, cottage cheese, natural yogurt and nutmeg together and pour over the cannelloni. Sprinkle with the grated mozzarella cheese and bake in the preheated oven for 15–20 minutes, or until the topping is golden brown and bubbling. Serve immediately with a tossed green salad.

Seared Tuna with Italian Salsa

SERVES 4

4 x 175 g/6 oz tuna or
   swordfish steaks
salt and freshly ground
   black pepper
3 tbsp Pernod
2 tbsp olive oil
zest and juice of 1 lemon
2 tsp fresh thyme leaves
2 tsp fennel seeds,
   lightly roasted

4 sun-dried tomatoes,
   chopped
1 tsp dried chilli flakes
assorted salad leaves,
   to serve

For the salsa:
1 white onion, peeled and
   finely chopped
2 tomatoes, deseeded

and sliced
2 tbsp freshly shredded
   basil leaves
1 red chilli, deseeded and
   finely sliced
3 tbsp extra-virgin olive oil
2 tsp balsamic vinegar
1 tsp caster sugar

Wipe the fish and season lightly with salt and pepper, then place in a shallow dish. Mix together the Pernod, olive oil, lemon zest and juice, thyme, fennel seeds, sun-dried tomatoes and chilli flakes and pour over the fish. Cover lightly and leave to marinate in a cool place for 1–2 hours, occasionally spooning the marinade over the fish.

Meanwhile, mix all the ingredients for the salsa together in a small bowl. Season to taste with salt and pepper, then cover and leave for about 30 minutes to allow all the flavours to develop.

Lightly oil a griddle pan and heat until hot. When the pan is very hot, drain the fish, reserving the marinade. Cook the fish for 3–4 minutes on each side, taking care not to overcook them – the tuna steaks should be a little pink inside. Pour any remaining marinade into a small saucepan, bring to the boil and boil for 1 minute. Serve the steaks hot with the marinade, chilled salsa and a few assorted salad leaves.

 Try this: FOR AN ALTERNATIVE: 104   FOR A LIGHT BITE: 34

Plaice with Parmesan & Anchovies

SERVES 4

4 plaice fillets
4 anchovy fillets,
    finely chopped
450 g/1 lb spinach, rinsed
3 firm tomatoes, sliced

200 ml/7 fl oz double cream
5 slices of olive
    ciabatta bread
50 g/2 oz wild rocket
8 tbsp Parmesan

cheese, grated
freshly cooked pasta,
    to serve

Preheat oven to 220°C/425°F/Gas Mark 7, 15 minutes before cooking. Put the plaice on a chopping board and holding the tail, strip off the skin from both sides. With a filleting knife, fillet the fish, then wipe and reserve.

Place the fillets on a large chopping board, skinned-side up and halve lengthways along the centre. Dot each one with some of the chopped anchovies, then roll up from the thickest end and reserve.

Pour boiling water over the spinach, leave for 2 minutes, drain, squeezing out as much moisture as possible, then place in the base of an ovenproof dish. Arrange the tomatoes on top of the spinach. Arrange the rolled-up fillets standing up in the dish and pour over the cream.

Place the ciabatta and rocket in a food processor and blend until finely chopped, then stir in the grated Parmesan cheese.

Sprinkle the topping over the fish and bake in the preheated oven for 8–10 minutes, or until the fish is cooked and has lost its translucency and the topping is golden brown. Serve with freshly cooked pasta.

Grilled Snapper with Roasted Pepper

SERVES 4

1 medium red pepper
1 medium green pepper
4–8 snapper fillets,
   depending on size,
   about 450 g/1 lb

sea salt and freshly ground
   black pepper
1 tbsp olive oil
5 tbsp double cream
125 ml/4 fl oz white wine

1 tbsp freshly chopped dill
sprigs of fresh dill,
   to garnish
freshly cooked tagliatelle,
   to serve

Preheat the grill to a high heat and line the grill rack with tinfoil. Cut the tops off the peppers and divide into quarters. Remove the seeds and the membrane, then place on the foil-lined grill rack and cook for 8–10 minutes, turning frequently, until the skins have become charred and blackened. Remove from the grill rack, place in a polythene bag and leave until cool. When the peppers are cool, strip off the skin, slice thinly and reserve.

Cover the grill rack with another piece of tinfoil, then place the snapper fillets skin-side up on the grill rack. Season to taste with salt and pepper and brush with a little of the olive oil. Cook for 10-12 minutes, turning over once and brushing again with a little olive oil.

Pour the cream and wine into a small saucepan, bring to the boil and simmer for about 5 minutes until the sauce has thickened slightly. Add the dill, season to taste and stir in the sliced peppers. Arrange the cooked snapper fillets on warm serving plates and pour over the cream and pepper sauce. Garnish with sprigs of dill and serve immediately with freshly cooked tagliatelle.

Try this: FOR AN ALTERNATIVE: 208 FOR A LIGHT BITE: 32

Pan-fried Salmon with Herb Risotto

SERVES 4

4 x 175 g/6 oz salmon fillets
3–4 tbsp plain flour
1 tsp dried mustard powder
salt and freshly ground
    black pepper
2 tbsp olive oil
3 shallots, peeled
    and chopped

225 g/8 oz Arborio rice
150 ml/¼ pint dry white wine
1.4 litres/2½ pints vegetable
    or fish stock
50 g/2 oz butter
2 tbsp freshly
    snipped chives
2 tbsp freshly chopped dill

2 tbsp freshly chopped
    flat-leaf parsley
knob of butter
slices of lemon, to garnish
sprigs of fresh dill,
    to garnish
tomato salad, to serve

Wipe the salmon fillets with a clean, damp cloth. Mix together the flour, mustard powder and seasoning on a large plate and use to coat the salmon fillets and reserve.

Heat half the olive oil in a large frying pan and fry the shallots for 5 minutes until softened, but not coloured. Add the rice and stir for 1 minute, then slowly add the wine, bring to the boil and boil rapidly until reduced by half.

Bring the stock to a gentle simmer, then add to the rice, a ladleful at a time. Cook, stirring frequently, until all the stock has been added and the rice is cooked but still retains a bite. Stir in the butter and freshly chopped herbs and season to taste with salt and pepper.

Heat the remaining olive oil and the knob of butter in a large griddle pan, add the salmon fillets and cook for 2–3 minutes on each side, or until cooked. Arrange the herb risotto on warm serving plates and top with the salmon. Garnish with slices of lemon and sprigs of dill and serve immediately with a tomato salad.

Try this: FOR AN ALTERNATIVE: 102 FOR A LIGHT BITE: 34

Marinated Mackerel with Tomato & Basil Salad

SERVES 3

3 mackerel, filleted
3 beefsteak tomatoes, sliced
50 g/2 oz watercress
2 oranges, peeled
  and segmented
75 g/3 oz mozzarella
  cheese, sliced
2 tbsp basil leaves, shredded

sprig of fresh basil,
  to garnish

For the marinade:
juice of 2 lemons
4 tbsp olive oil
4 tbsp basil leaves

For the dressing:
1 tbsp lemon juice
1 tsp Dijon mustard
1 tsp caster sugar
salt and freshly ground
  black pepper
5 tbsp olive oil

Remove as many of the fine pin bones as possible from the mackerel fillets, lightly rinse and pat dry with absorbent kitchen paper and place in a shallow dish.

Blend the marinade ingredients together and pour over the mackerel fillets. Make sure the marinade has covered the fish completely. Cover and leave in a cool place for at least 8 hours, but preferably overnight. As the fillets marinate, they will loose the translucency and look as if they are cooked.

Place the tomatoes, watercress, oranges and mozzarella cheese in a large bowl and toss.

To make the dressing, whisk the lemon juice with the mustard, sugar and seasoning in a bowl. Pour over half the dressing, toss again and then arrange on a serving platter. Remove the mackerel from the marinade, cut into bite-sized pieces and sprinkle with the shredded basil. Arrange on top of the salad, drizzle over the remaining dressing, scatter with basil leaves and garnish with a basil sprig. Serve.

Try this: FOR AN ALTERNATIVE: 114 FOR A LIGHT BITE: 30

Pappardelle with Smoked Haddock & Blue Cheese Sauce

SERVES 4

350 g/12 oz smoked haddock
2 bay leaves
300 ml/½ pint milk
400 g/14 oz pappardelle
 or tagliatelle
25 g/1 oz butter
25 g/1 oz plain flour

150 ml/¼ pint single cream
 or extra milk
125 g/4 oz Dolcelatte cheese
 or Gorgonzola, cut into
 small pieces
¼ tsp freshly grated nutmeg
salt and freshly ground

black pepper
40 g/1½ oz toasted
 walnuts, chopped
1 tbsp freshly
 chopped parsley

Place the smoked haddock in a saucepan with 1 bay leaf and pour in the milk. Bring to the boil slowly, cover and simmer for 6–7 minutes, or until the fish is opaque. Remove and roughly flake the fish, discarding the skin and any bones. Strain the milk and reserve.

Bring a large pan of lightly salted water to a rolling boil. Add the pasta and cook according to the packet instructions, or until 'al dente'.

Meanwhile, place the butter, flour and single cream or milk if preferred, in a pan and stir to mix. Stir in the reserved warm milk and add the remaining bay leaf. Bring to the boil, whisking all the time until smooth and thick. Gently simmer for 3–4 minutes, stirring frequently. Discard the bay leaf.

Add the Dolcelatte or Gorgonzola cheese to the sauce. Heat gently, stirring until melted. Add the flaked haddock and season to taste with nutmeg and salt and pepper.

Drain the pasta thoroughly and return to the pan. Add the sauce and toss gently to coat, taking care not to break up the flakes of fish. Tip into a warmed serving bowl, sprinkle with toasted walnuts and parsley and serve immediately.

Try this: FOR AN ALTERNATIVE: 276 FOR A LIGHT BITE: 52

Seared Salmon & Lemon Linguine

SERVES 4

4 small skinless salmon
fillets, each about
75 g/3 oz
2 tsp sunflower oil
½ tsp mixed or black
peppercorns, crushed

400 g/14 oz linguine
15 g/½ oz unsalted butter
1 bunch spring onions,
trimmed and shredded
300 ml/½ pint soured cream
zest of 1 lemon, finely grated

50 g/2 oz freshly grated
Parmesan cheese
1 tbsp lemon juice
pinch of salt
dill sprigs, to garnish
lemon slices, to garnish

Brush the salmon fillets with the sunflower oil, sprinkle with crushed peppercorns and press on firmly and reserve.

Bring a large pan of lightly salted water to a rolling boil. Add the linguine and cook according to the packet instructions, or until 'al dente'.

Meanwhile, melt the butter in a saucepan and cook the shredded spring onions gently for 2–3 minutes, or until soft. Stir in the soured cream and the lemon zest and remove from the heat.

Preheat a griddle or heavy-based frying pan until very hot. Add the salmon and sear for 1½–2 minutes on each side. Remove from the pan and allow to cool slightly.

Bring the soured cream sauce to the boil and stir in the Parmesan cheese and lemon juice. Drain the pasta thoroughly and return to the pan. Pour over the sauce and toss gently to coat.

Spoon the pasta on to warmed serving plates and top with the salmon fillets. Serve immediately with sprigs of dill and lemon slices.

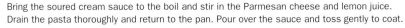

Try this: FOR AN ALTERNATIVE: 188   FOR A LIGHT BITE: 38

Tagliatelle with Tuna & Anchovy Tapenade

SERVES 4

400 g/14 oz tagliatelle
125 g can tuna fish in
   oil, drained
45 g/1¾ oz can anchovy
   fillets, drained

150 g/5 oz pitted black olives
2 tbsp capers in
   brine, drained
2 tsp lemon juice
100 ml/3½ fl oz olive oil

2 tbsp freshly
   chopped parsley
freshly ground black pepper
sprigs of flat-leaf parsley,
   to garnish

Bring a large pan of lightly salted water to a rolling boil. Add the tagliatelle and cook according to the packet instructions, or until 'al dente'.

Meanwhile, place the tuna fish, anchovy fillets, olives and capers in a food processor with the lemon juice and 2 tablespoons of the olive oil and blend for a few seconds until roughly chopped.

With the motor running, pour in the remaining olive oil in a steady stream; the resulting mixture should be slightly chunky rather than smooth.

Spoon the sauce into a bowl, stir in the chopped parsley and season to taste with black pepper. Check the taste of the sauce and add a little more lemon juice, if required.

Drain the pasta thoroughly. Pour the sauce into the pan and cook over a low heat for 1–2 minutes to warm through.

Return the drained pasta to the pan and mix together with the sauce. Tip into a warmed serving bowl or spoon on to warm individual plates. Garnish with sprigs of flat-leaf parsley and serve immediately.

Try this: FOR AN ALTERNATIVE: 120   FOR A LIGHT BITE: 32

Pan–fried Scallops & Pasta

SERVES 4

16 large scallops, shelled
1 tbsp olive oil
1 garlic clove, peeled
    and crushed
1 tsp freshly chopped thyme
400 g/14 oz penne
4 sun-dried tomatoes in oil,
    drained and thinly sliced

thyme or oregano sprigs,
    to garnish

For the tomato dressing:
2 sun-dried tomatoes in oil,
    drained and chopped
1 tbsp red wine vinegar
2 tsp balsamic vinegar

1 tsp sun-dried tomato paste
1 tsp caster sugar
salt and freshly ground
    black pepper
2 tbsp oil from a jar of
    sun-dried tomatoes
2 tbsp olive oil

Rinse the scallops and pat dry on absorbent kitchen paper. Place in a bowl and add the olive oil, crushed garlic and thyme. Cover and chill in the refrigerator until ready to cook.

Bring a large pan of lightly salted water to a rolling boil. Add the penne and cook according to the packet instructions, or until 'al dente'.

Meanwhile, make the dressing. Place the sun-dried tomatoes into a small bowl or glass jar and add the vinegars, tomato paste, sugar, salt and pepper. Whisk well, then pour into a food processor. With the motor running, pour in the sun-dried tomato oil and olive oil in a steady stream to make a thick, smooth dressing.

Preheat a large, dry cast-iron griddle pan over a high heat for about 5 minutes. Lower the heat to medium then add the scallops to the pan. Cook for 1½ minutes on each side. Remove from the pan.

Drain the pasta thoroughly and return to the pan. Add the sliced sun-dried tomatoes and dressing and toss. Divide between individual serving plates, top each portion with 4 scallops, garnish with fresh thyme or oregano sprigs and serve immediately.

Try this: FOR AN ALTERNATIVE: 76 FOR A LIGHT BITE: 68

Smoked Mackerel & Pasta Frittata

SERVES 4

25 g/1 oz tricolore pasta
    spirals or shells
225 g/8 oz smoked mackerel
6 medium eggs
3 tbsp milk
2 tsp wholegrain mustard
2 tbsp freshly

chopped parsley
salt and freshly ground
    black pepper
25 g/1 oz unsalted butter
6 spring onions, trimmed
    and diagonally sliced
50 g/2 oz frozen

peas, thawed
75 g/3 oz mature Cheddar
    cheese, grated
green salad, to serve
warm crusty bread, to serve

Preheat the grill to high just before cooking. Bring a pan of lightly salted water to a rolling boil. Add the pasta and cook according to the packet instructions, or until 'al dente'. Drain thoroughly and reserve.

Remove the skin from the mackerel and break the fish into large flakes, discarding any bones, and reserve. Place the eggs, milk, mustard and parsley in a bowl and whisk together. Season with just a little salt and plenty of freshly ground black pepper and reserve.

Melt the butter in a large, heavy-based frying pan. Cook the spring onions gently for 3–4 minutes, until soft. Pour in the egg mixture, then add the drained pasta, peas and half of the mackerel.

Gently stir the mixture in the pan for 1–2 minutes, or until beginning to set. Stop stirring and cook for about 1 minute until the underneath is golden-brown.

Scatter the remaining mackerel over the frittata, followed by the grated cheese. Place under the preheated grill for about 1½ minutes, or until golden-brown and set. Cut into wedges and serve immediately with salad and crusty bread.

Try this: FOR AN ALTERNATIVE: 98 FOR A LIGHT BITE: 32

Crispy Cod Cannelloni

SERVES 4

1 tbsp olive oil
8 dried cannelloni tubes
25 g/1 oz unsalted butter
225 g/8 oz button
    mushrooms, thinly sliced
175 g/6 oz leeks, trimmed
    and finely chopped

175 g/6 oz cod, skinned
    and diced
175 g/6 oz cream cheese
salt and freshly ground
    black pepper
15 g/½ oz Parmesan
    cheese, grated

50 g/2 oz fine fresh white
    breadcrumbs
3 tbsp plain flour
1 medium egg, lightly beaten
oil for deep frying
fresh herbs or salad leaves,
    to serve

Add 1 teaspoon of the olive oil to a large pan of lightly salted water and bring to a rolling boil. Add the cannelloni tubes and cook, uncovered, for 5 minutes. Drain and leave in a bowl of cold water.

Melt the butter with the remaining oil in a saucepan. Add the mushrooms and leeks and cook gently for 5 minutes. Turn up the heat and cook for 1–2 minutes, or until the mixture is fairly dry. Add the cod and cook, stirring, for 2–3 minutes, or until the fish is opaque. Add the cream cheese to the pan and stir until melted. Season to taste with salt and pepper, then leave the cod mixture to cool.

Drain the cannelloni. Using a piping bag without a nozzle or a spoon, fill the cannelloni with the cod mixture. Mix the Parmesan cheese and breadcrumbs together on a plate. Dip the filled cannelloni into the flour, then into the beaten egg and finally into the breadcrumb mixture. Dip the ends twice to ensure they are thoroughly coated. Chill in the refrigerator for 30 minutes.

Heat the oil for deep frying to 180°C/350°F. Fry the stuffed cannelloni in batches for 2–3 minutes, or until the coating is crisp and golden-brown. Drain on absorbent kitchen paper and serve immediately with fresh herbs or salad leaves.

 Try this: FOR AN ALTERNATIVE: 88 FOR A LIGHT BITE: 38

Spaghetti alle Vongole

SERVES 4

1.8 kg/4 lb small fresh clams	2 garlic cloves, peeled	2 tbsp freshly chopped or
6 tbsp dry white wine	and crushed	torn basil
2 tbsp olive oil	400 g/14 oz spaghetti	salt and freshly ground
1 small onion, peeled and	2 tbsp freshly	black pepper
finely chopped	chopped parsley	oregano leaves, to garnish

Soak the clams in lightly salted cold water for 8 hours before required, changing the water once or twice. Scrub the clams, removing any that have broken shells or that remain open when tapped. Place the prepared clams in a large saucepan and pour in the wine. Cover with a tight-fitting lid and cook over a medium heat for 5–6 minutes, shaking the pan occasionally, until the shells have opened.

Strain the clams and cooking juices through a sieve lined with muslin and reserve. Discard any clams that have remained unopened. Heat the olive oil in a saucepan and fry the onion and garlic gently for 10 minutes, or until very soft.

Meanwhile, bring a large pan of lightly salted water to a rolling boil. Add the spaghetti and cook according to the packet instructions, or until 'al dente'.

Add the cooked clams to the onions and garlic and pour in the reserved cooking juices. Bring to the boil, then add the parsley and basil and season to taste with salt and black pepper.

Drain the spaghetti thoroughly. Return to the pan and add the clams with their sauce. Toss together gently, then tip into a large warmed serving bowl or into individual bowls. Serve immediately, sprinkled with oregano leaves.

Try this: FOR AN ALTERNATIVE: 116   FOR A LIGHT BITE: 68

Pasta & Mussels in Tomato & Wine Sauce

SERVES 4

900 g/2 lb fresh live mussels
1 bay leaf
150 ml/¼ pint light red wine
15 g/½ oz unsalted butter
1 tbsp olive oil
1 red onion, peeled and
   thinly sliced

2 garlic cloves, peeled
   and crushed
550 g/1¼ lb ripe tomatoes,
   skinned, deseeded
   and chopped
400 g/14 oz fiochetti
   or penne

3 tbsp freshly chopped or
   torn basil
salt and freshly ground
   black pepper
basil leaves, to garnish
crusty bread, to serve

Scrub the mussels and remove any beards. Discard any that do not close when lightly tapped. Place in a large pan with the bay leaf and pour in the wine. Cover with a tight-fitting lid and steam, shaking the pan occasionally, for 3–4 minutes, or until the mussels open. Remove the mussels with a slotted spoon, discarding any that have not opened, and reserve. Strain the cooking liquid through a muslin-lined sieve and reserve.

Melt the butter with the oil in a large saucepan and gently cook the onion and garlic for 10 minutes, until soft. Add the reserved cooking liquid and the tomatoes and simmer, uncovered, for 6–7 minutes, or until very soft and the sauce has reduced slightly.

Meanwhile, bring a large pan of lightly salted water to a rolling boil. Add the pasta and cook acording to the packet instructions, or until 'al dente'.

Drain the pasta thoroughly and return to the pan. Add the mussels, removing the shells if you prefer, with the tomato sauce. Stir in the basil and season to taste with salt and pepper. Toss together gently. Tip into warmed serving bowls, garnish with basil leaves and serve with crusty bread.

Salmon & Spaghetti in a Creamy Egg Sauce

SERVES 4

3 medium eggs
1 tbsp freshly
   chopped parsley
1 tbsp freshly chopped dill
40 g/1½ oz freshly grated
   Parmesan cheese

40 g/1½ oz freshly grated
   pecorino cheese
2 tbsp dry white wine
freshly ground black pepper
400 g/14 oz spaghetti
350 g/12 oz salmon

   fillet, skinned
25 g/1 oz butter
1 tsp olive oil
flat-leaf parsley sprigs,
   to garnish

Beat the eggs in a bowl with the parsley, dill, half of the Parmesan and pecorino cheeses and the white wine. Season to taste with freshly ground black pepper and reserve.

Bring a large pan of lightly salted water to a rolling boil. Add the spaghetti and cook according to the packet instructions, or until 'al dente'.

Meanwhile, cut the salmon into bite-sized pieces. Melt the butter in a large frying pan with the oil and cook the salmon pieces for 3–4 minutes, or until opaque.

Drain the spaghetti thoroughly, return to the pan and immediately add the egg mixture. Remove from the heat and toss well; the eggs will cook in the heat of the spaghetti to make a creamy sauce.

Stir in the remaining cheeses and the cooked pieces of salmon and toss again. Tip into a warmed serving bowl or on to individual plates. Garnish with sprigs of flat-leaf parsley and serve immediately.

Try this: FOR AN ALTERNATIVE: 190   FOR A LIGHT BITE: 48

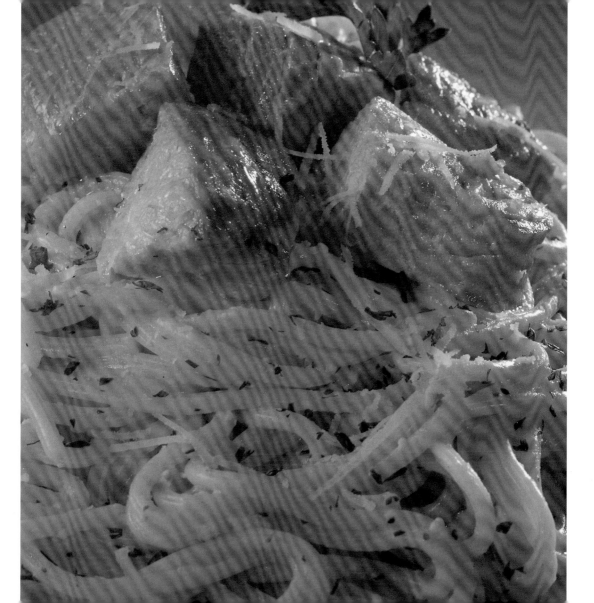

Creamy Coconut Seafood Pasta

SERVES 4

400 g/14 oz egg tagliatelle
1 tsp sunflower oil
1 tsp sesame oil
4 spring onions, trimmed
    and sliced diagonally
1 garlic clove, peeled
    and crushed
1 red chilli, deseeded and
finely chopped
2.5 cm/1 inch piece fresh
    root ginger, peeled
    and grated
150 ml/¼ pint coconut milk
100 ml/3½ fl oz
    double cream
225 g/8 oz cooked peeled
tiger prawns
185 g/6½ oz fresh white
    crab meat
2 tbsp freshly chopped
    coriander, plus sprigs
    to garnish
salt and freshly ground
    black pepper

Bring a large pan of lightly salted water to a rolling boil. Add the pasta and cook according to the packet instructions, or until 'al dente'.

Meanwhile, heat the sunflower and sesame oils together in a saucepan. Add the spring onions, garlic, chilli and ginger and cook for 3–4 minutes, or until softened.

Blend the coconut milk and cream together in a jug. Add the prawns and crab meat to the pan and stir over a low heat for a few seconds to heat through. Gradually pour in the coconut cream, stirring all the time.

Stir the chopped coriander into the seafood sauce and season to taste with salt and pepper. Continue heating the sauce gently until piping hot, but do not allow to boil.

Drain the pasta thoroughly and return to the pan. Add the seafood sauce and gently toss together to coat the pasta. Tip into a warmed serving dish or spoon on to individual plates. Serve immediately, garnished with fresh coriander sprigs.

Try this: FOR AN ALTERNATIVE : 116 FOR A LIGHT BITE: 40

Fettuccine with Sardines & Spinach

SERVES 4

120g can sardines in olive oil
400 g/14 oz fettuccine or
   tagliarini
40 g/1½ oz butter
2 tbsp olive oil
50 g/2 oz one-day-old white
   breadcrumbs

1 garlic clove, peeled and
   finely chopped
50 g/2 oz pine nuts
125 g/4 oz chestnut
   mushrooms, wiped and
   sliced
125 g/4 oz baby spinach

leaves, rinsed
150 ml/¼ pint crème fraîche
rind of 1 lemon, finely
   grated
salt and freshly ground black
   pepper

Drain the sardines and cut in half lengthwise. Remove the bones, then cut the fish into 2.5 cm/1 inch pieces and reserve.

Bring a large pan of lightly salted water to a rolling boil. Add the pasta and cook according to the packet instructions, or until 'al dente'.

Meanwhile, melt half the butter with the olive oil in a large saucepan, add the breadcrumbs and fry, stirring, until they begin to turn crisp. Add the garlic and pine nuts and continue to cook until golden-brown. Remove from the pan and reserve. Wipe the pan clean.

Melt the remaining butter in the pan, add the mushrooms and cook for 4–5 minutes, or until soft. Add the spinach and cook, stirring, for 1 minute, or until beginning to wilt. Stir in the crème fraîche and lemon rind and bring to the boil. Simmer gently until the spinach is just cooked. Season the sauce to taste with salt and pepper.

Drain the pasta thoroughly and return to the pan. Add the spinach sauce and sardine pieces and gently toss together. Tip into a warmed serving dish. Sprinkle with the toasted breadcrumbs and pine nuts and serve immediately.

Try this: FOR AN ALTERNATIVE : 104 FOR A LIGHT BITE: 32

Warm Swordfish Niçoise

SERVES 4

4 swordfish steaks, about 2.5 cm/1 inch thick, weighing about 175 g/6 oz each	400 g/14 oz farfalle	225 g/8 oz ripe tomatoes, quartered
juice of 1 lime	225 g/8 oz French beans, topped and cut in half	50 g/2 oz pitted black olives
2 tbsp olive oil	1 tsp Dijon mustard	2 medium eggs, hard boiled and quartered
salt and freshly ground black pepper	2 tsp white wine vinegar	8 anchovy fillets, drained and cut in half lengthways
	pinch caster sugar	
	3 tbsp olive oil	

Place the swordfish steaks in a shallow dish. Mix the lime juice with the oil, season to taste with salt and pepper and spoon over the steaks. Turn the steaks to coat them evenly. Cover and place in the refrigerator to marinate for 1 hour.

Bring a large pan of lightly salted water to a rolling boil. Add the farfalle and cook according to the packet instructions, or until 'al dente'. Add the French beans about 4 minutes before the end of cooking time.

Mix the mustard, vinegar and sugar together in a small jug. Gradually whisk in the olive oil to make a thick dressing.

Cook the swordfish in a griddle pan or under a hot preheated grill for 2 minutes on each side, or until just cooked through; overcooking will make it tough and dry. Remove and cut into 2 cm/¾ inch chunks.

Drain the pasta and beans thoroughly and place in a large bowl. Pour over the dressing and toss to coat. Add the cooked swordfish, tomatoes, olives, hard-boiled eggs and anchovy fillets. Gently toss together, taking care not to break up the eggs. Tip into a warmed serving bowl or divide the pasta between individual plates. Serve immediately.

Try this: FOR AN ALTERNATIVE : 244 FOR A LIGHT BITE: 46

Meats

Oven–roasted Vegetables with Sausages

SERVES 4

2 medium aubergines, trimmed
3 medium courgettes, trimmed
4 tbsp olive oil
6 garlic cloves

8 Tuscany-style sausages
4 plum tomatoes
2 x 300 g cans cannellini beans
salt and freshly ground black pepper

1 bunch of fresh basil, torn into coarse pieces
4 tbsp Parmesan cheese, grated

Preheat oven to 200°C/400°F/Gas Mark 6, 15 minutes before cooking. Cut the aubergines and courgettes into bite-sized chunks. Place the olive oil in a large roasting tin and heat in the preheated oven for 3 minutes, or until very hot. Add the aubergines, courgettes and garlic cloves, then stir until coated in the hot oil and cook in the oven for 10 minutes.

Remove the roasting tin from the oven and stir. Lightly prick the sausages, add to the roasting tin and return to the oven. Continue to roast for a further 20 minutes, turning once during cooking, until the vegetables are tender and the sausages are golden brown.

Meanwhile, roughly chop the plum tomatoes and drain the cannellini beans. Remove the sausages from the oven and stir in the tomatoes and cannellini beans. Season to taste with salt and pepper, then return to the oven for 5 minutes, or until heated thoroughly.

Scatter over the basil leaves and sprinkle with plenty of Parmesan cheese and extra freshly ground black pepper. Serve immediately.

Try this: FOR AN ALTERNATIVE: 224 FOR A LIGHT BITE: 20

Italian Risotto

SERVES 4

1 onion, peeled
2 garlic cloves, peeled
1 tbsp olive oil
125 g/4 oz Italian salami or
   speck, chopped
125 g/4 oz asparagus
350 g/12 oz risotto rice

300 ml/½ pt dry white wine
1 litre/1¾ pints chicken
   stock, warmed
125g/4 oz frozen broad
   beans, defrosted
125g/4 oz Dolcelatte
   cheese, diced

3 tbsp freshly chopped
   mixed herbs, such as
   parsley and basil
salt and freshly ground
   black pepper

Chop the onion and garlic and reserve. Heat the olive oil in a large frying pan and cook the salami for 3–5 minutes, or until golden. Using a slotted spoon, transfer to a plate and keep warm. Add the asparagus and stir-fry for 2–3 minutes, until just wilted. Transfer to the plate with the salami. Add the onion and garlic and cook for 5 minutes, or until softened.

Add the rice to the pan and cook for about 2 minutes. Add the wine, bring to the boil, then simmer, stirring until the wine has been absorbed. Add half the stock and return to the boil. Simmer, stirring until the liquid has been absorbed.

Add half of the remaining stock and the broad beans to the rice mixture. Bring to the boil, then simmer for a further 5–10 minutes, or until all of the liquid has been absorbed.

Add the remaining stock, bring to the boil, then simmer until all the liquid is absorbed and the rice is tender. Stir in the remaining ingredients until the cheese has just melted. Serve immediately.

Pan–fried Beef with Creamy Mushrooms

SERVES 4

225 g/8 oz shallots, peeled
2 garlic cloves, peeled
2 tbsp olive oil
4 medallions of beef
4 plum tomatoes

125 g/4 oz flat mushrooms
3 tbsp brandy
150 ml/¼ pint red wine
salt and freshly ground
    black pepper

4 tbsp double cream
baby new potatoes, to serve
freshly cooked green beans,
    to serve

Cut the shallots in half if large, then chop the garlic. Heat the oil in a large frying pan and cook the shallots for about 8 minutes, stirring occasionally, until almost softened. Add the garlic and beef and cook for 8–10 minutes, turning once during cooking until the meat is browned all over. Using a slotted spoon, transfer the beef to a plate and keep warm.

Rinse the tomatoes and cut into eighths, then wipe the mushrooms and slice. Add to the pan and cook for 5 minutes, stirring frequently until the mushrooms have softened.

Pour in the brandy and heat through. Draw the pan off the heat and carefully ignite. Allow the flames to subside. Pour in the wine, return to the heat and bring to the boil. Boil until reduced by one-third. Draw the pan off the heat, season to taste with salt and pepper, add the cream and stir.

Arrange the beef on serving plates and spoon over the sauce. Serve with baby new potatoes and a few green beans.

Try this: FOR AN ALTERNATIVE: 172 FOR A LIGHT BITE: 64

Spaghetti Bolognese

SERVES 4

1 carrot
2 celery stalks
1 onion
2 garlic cloves
450 g/1 lb lean minced
    beef steak
225 g/8 oz smoked streaky

bacon, chopped
1 tbsp plain flour
150 ml/¼ pint red wine
379 g can chopped tomatoes
2 tbsp tomato purée
2 tsp dried mixed herbs
salt and freshly ground

black pepper
pinch of sugar
350 g/12 oz spaghetti
sprigs of fresh oregano,
    to garnish
shavings of Parmesan
    cheese, to serve

Peel and chop the carrot, trim and chop the celery, then peel and chop the onion and garlic. Heat a large non-stick frying pan and sauté the beef and bacon for 5–10 minutes, stirring occasionally, until browned. Add the prepared vegetables to the frying pan and cook for about 3 minutes, or until softened, stirring occasionally.

Add the flour and cook for 1 minute. Stir in the red wine, tomatoes, tomato purée, mixed herbs, seasoning to taste and sugar. Bring to the boil, then cover and simmer for 45 minutes, stirring occasionally.

Meanwhile, bring a large saucepan of lightly salted water to the boil and cook the spaghetti for 10–12 minutes, or until 'al dente'. Drain well and divide between 4 serving plates. Spoon over the sauce, garnish with a few sprigs of oregano and serve immediately with plenty of Parmesan shavings.

Try this: FOR AN ALTERNATIVE: 150   FOR A LIGHT BITE: 36

Meatballs with Olives

SERVES 4

250 g/9 oz shallots, peeled
2–3 garlic cloves, peeled
450 g/1 lb minced beef steak
2 tbsp fresh white or
    wholemeal breadcrumbs
3 tbsp freshly chopped basil
salt and freshly ground
    black pepper

2 tbsp olive oil
5 tbsp ready-made
    pesto sauce
5 tbsp mascarpone cheese
50 g/2 oz pitted black
    olives, halved
275 g/10 oz thick pasta
    noodles

freshly chopped flat-leaf
    parsley
sprigs of fresh flat-leaf
    parsley, to garnish
freshly grated Parmesan
    cheese, to serve

Chop 2 of the shallots finely and place in a bowl with the garlic, beef, breadcrumbs, basil and seasoning to taste. With damp hands, bring the mixture together and shape into small balls about the size of an apricot.

Heat the olive oil in a frying pan and cook the meatballs for 8–10 minutes, turning occasionally, until browned and the beef is tender. Remove and drain on absorbent kitchen paper.

Slice the remaining shallots, add to the pan and cook for 5 minutes, until softened. Blend the pesto and mascarpone together, then stir into the pan with the olives. Bring to the boil, reduce the heat and return the meatballs to the pan. Simmer for 5–8 minutes, or until the sauce has thickened and the meatballs are cooked thoroughly.

Meanwhile, bring a large saucepan of lightly salted water to the boil and cook the noodles for 8–10 minutes, or 'al dente'. Drain the noodles, reserving 2 tablespoons of the cooking liquor. Return the noodles to the pan with the cooking liquor and pour in the sauce. Stir the noodles, then sprinkle with chopped parsley. Garnish with a few sprigs of parsley and serve immediately with grated Parmesan cheese.

Try this: FOR AN ALTERNATIVE: 152 FOR A LIGHT BITE: 26

Traditional Lasagne

SERVES 4

450 g/1 lb lean minced
  beef steak
175 g/6 oz pancetta or
  smoked streaky
  bacon, chopped
1 large onion, peeled
  and chopped
2 celery stalks, trimmed
  and chopped
125 g/4 oz button mushrooms,
  wiped and chopped

2 garlic cloves, peeled
  and chopped
90 g/3½ oz plain flour
300 ml/½ pint beef stock
1 tbsp freeze-dried mixed
  herbs
5 tbsp tomato purée
salt and freshly ground
  black pepper
75 g/3 oz butter
1 tsp English mustard powder

pinch of freshly grated nutmeg
900 ml/1½ pints milk
125 g/4 oz Parmesan
  cheese, grated
125 g/4 oz Cheddar
  cheese, grated
8–12 precooked lasagne
  sheets
crusty bread, to serve
fresh green salad leaves,
  to serve

Preheat oven to 200°C/400°F/Gas Mark 6, 15 minutes before cooking. Cook the beef and pancetta in a large saucepan for 10 minutes, stirring to break up any lumps. Add the onion, celery and mushrooms and cook for 4 minutes, or until softened slightly. Stir in the garlic and 1 tablespoon of the flour, then cook for 1 minute. Stir in the stock, herbs and tomato purée. Season to taste with salt and pepper. Bring to the boil, then cover, reduce the heat and simmer for 45 minutes.

Meanwhile, melt the butter in a small saucepan and stir in the remaining flour, mustard powder and nutmeg, until well blended. Cook for 2 minutes. Remove from the heat and gradually blend in the milk until smooth. Return to the heat and bring to the boil, stirring, until thickened. Gradually stir in half the Parmesan and Cheddar cheeses until melted. Season to taste.

Spoon half the meat mixture into the base of a large ovenproof dish. Top with a single layer of pasta. Spread over half the sauce and scatter with half the cheese. Repeat layers finishing with cheese. Bake in the preheated oven for 30 minutes, or until the pasta is cooked and the top is golden brown and bubbly. Serve immediately with crusty bread and a green salad.

Try this: FOR AN ALTERNATIVE: 280 FOR A LIGHT BITE: 20

Fillet Steaks with Tomato & Garlic Sauce

SERVES 4

700 g/1½ lb ripe tomatoes	oregano	olives, chopped
2 garlic cloves	2 tbsp red wine	4 fillet steaks, about
2 tbsp olive oil	salt and freshly ground	175 g/6 oz each in weight
2 tbsp freshly chopped basil	black pepper	freshly cooked vegetables,
2 tbsp freshly chopped	75 g/3 oz pitted black	to serve

Make a small cross on the top of each tomato and place in a large bowl. Cover with boiling water and leave for 2 minutes. Using a slotted spoon, remove the tomatoes and skin carefully. Repeat until all the tomatoes are skinned. Place on a chopping board, cut into quarters, remove the seeds and roughly chop, then reserve.

Peel and chop the garlic. Heat half the olive oil in a saucepan and cook the garlic for 30 seconds. Add the chopped tomatoes with the basil, oregano, red wine and season to taste with salt and pepper. Bring to the boil then reduce the heat, cover and simmer for 15 minutes, stirring occasionally, or until the sauce is reduced and thickened. Stir the olives into the sauce and keep warm while cooking the steaks.

Meanwhile, lightly oil a griddle pan or heavy-based frying pan with the remaining olive oil and cook the steaks for 2 minutes on each side to seal. Continue to cook the steaks for a further 2–4 minutes, depending on personal preference. Serve the steaks immediately with the garlic sauce and freshly cooked vegetables.

Try this: FOR AN ALTERNATIVE: 176 FOR A LIGHT BITE: 34

Cannelloni

SERVES 4

2 tbsp olive oil
175 g/6 oz fresh pork mince
75 g/3 oz chicken livers,
　chopped
1 small onion, peeled
　and chopped
1 garlic clove, peeled
　and chopped
175 g/6 oz frozen chopped

spinach, thawed
1 tbsp freeze-dried oregano
pinch of freshly grated
　nutmeg
salt and freshly ground
　black pepper
175 g/6 oz ricotta cheese
25 g/1 oz butter
25 g/1 oz plain flour

600 ml/1 pint milk
600 ml/1 pint ready-made
　tomato sauce
16 precooked
　cannelloni tubes
50 g/2 oz Parmesan
　cheese, grated
green salad, to serve

Preheat oven to 190°C/375°F/Gas Mark 5, 10 minutes before cooking. Heat the olive oil in a frying pan and cook the mince and chicken livers for about 5 minutes, stirring occasionally, until browned all over. Break up any lumps if necessary with a wooden spoon.

Add the onion and garlic and cook for 4 minutes, until softened. Add the spinach, oregano, nutmeg and season to taste with salt and pepper. Cook until all the liquid has evaporated, then remove the pan from the heat and allow to cool. Stir in the ricotta cheese.

Meanwhile, melt the butter in a small saucepan and stir in the plain flour to form a roux. Cook for 2 minutes, stirring occasionally. Remove from the heat and blend in the milk until smooth. Return to the heat and bring to the boil, stirring until the sauce has thickened. Reserve.

Spoon a thin layer of the tomato sauce on the base of a large ovenproof dish. Divide the pork filling between the cannelloni tubes. Arrange on top of the tomato sauce. Spoon over the remaining tomato sauce. Pour over the white sauce and sprinkle with the Parmesan cheese. Bake in the preheated oven for 30–35 minutes, or until the cannelloni is tender and the top is golden brown. Serve immediately with a green salad.

Try this: FOR AN ALTERNATIVE: 88 FOR A LIGHT BITE: 28

Vitello Tonnato
(Veal in Tuna Sauce)

SERVES 6-8

900g/2 lb boned, rolled leg
  or loin of veal
300 ml/½ pint dry white wine
1 onion, peeled and
  chopped
1 carrot, peeled and
  chopped
2 celery stalks, trimmed

and chopped
1 bay leaf
2 garlic cloves few sprigs
  of parsley
salt and freshly ground
  black pepper
200 g can tuna in oil
2 tbsp capers, drained

6 anchovy fillets
200 ml/7 fl oz mayonnaise
  juice of ½ lemon
lemon wedges capers black
  olives, to garnish
fresh green salad leaves,
  to serve
tomato wedges, to serve

Place the veal in a large bowl and pour over the wine. Add the onion, carrot, celery, bay leaf, garlic cloves, parsley, salt and pepper. Cover tightly and chill overnight in the refrigerator. Transfer the contents of the bowl to a large saucepan, add just enough water to cover the meat. Bring to the boil, cover and simmer for 1–1¼ hours, or until the veal is tender.

Remove from the heat and allow the veal to cool in the juices. Using a slotted spoon, transfer the veal to a plate, pat dry with absorbent kitchen paper and reserve.

Place the tuna, capers, anchovy fillets, mayonnaise and lemon juice in a food processor or liquidiser and blend until smooth, adding a few spoonfuls of the pan juices to make the sauce of a coating consistency, if necessary. Season to taste with salt and pepper.

Using a sharp knife slice the veal thinly and arrange on a large serving platter.

Spoon the sauce over the veal. Cover with clingfilm and chill in the refrigerator overnight. Garnish with lemon wedges, capers and olives. Serve with salad and tomato wedges.

Try this: FOR AN ALTERNATIVE: 90 FOR A LIGHT BITE: 20

Italian Beef Pot Roast

SERVES 6

1.8 kg/4 lb brisket of beef	450 g/1 lb ripe tomatoes	salt and freshly ground
225 g/8 oz small onions,	300 ml/½ pint Italian	black pepper
peeled	red wine	25 g/1 oz butter
3 garlic cloves, peeled	2 tbsp olive oil	25 g/1 oz plain flour
and chopped	300 ml/½ pint beef stock	freshly cooked vegetables,
2 celery sticks, trimmed	1 tbsp tomato purée	to serve
and chopped	2 tsp freeze-dried	
2 carrots, peeled and sliced	mixed herbs	

Preheat oven to 150°C/300°F/Gas Mark 2, 10 minutes before cooking. Place the beef in a bowl. Add the onions, garlic, celery and carrots. Place the tomatoes in a bowl and cover with boiling water. Allow to stand for 2 minutes and drain. Peel away the skins, discard the seeds and chop, then add to the bowl with the red wine. Cover tightly and marinate in the refrigerator overnight.

Lift the marinated beef from the bowl and pat dry with absorbent kitchen paper. Heat the olive oil in a large casserole dish and cook the beef until it is browned all over, then remove. Drain the vegetables from the marinade, reserving the marinade. Add the vegetables to the casserole dish and fry gently for 5 minutes, stirring occasionally, until all the vegetables are browned.

Return the beef to the casserole dish with the marinade, beef stock, tomato purée, mixed herbs and season with salt and pepper. Bring to the boil, then cover and cook in the preheated oven for 3 hours.

Using a slotted spoon transfer the beef and any large vegetables to a plate and leave in a warm place. Blend the butter and flour to form a paste. Bring the casserole juices to the boil and then gradually stir in small spoonfuls of the paste. Cook until thickened. Serve with the sauce and a selection of vegetables.

Try this: FOR AN ALTERNATIVE: 178 FOR A LIGHT BITE: 36

Italian Meatballs in Tomato Sauce

SERVES 4

For the tomato sauce:
4 tbsp olive oil
1 large onion, peeled and
    finely chopped
2 garlic cloves, peeled
    and chopped
400 g can chopped tomatoes
1 tbsp sun-dried
    tomato paste

1 tbsp dried mixed herbs
150 ml/¼ pint red wine
salt and freshly ground
    black pepper

For the meatballs:
450 g/1 lb fresh pork mince
50 g/2 oz fresh breadcrumbs
1 medium egg yolk

75 g/3 oz Parmesan
    cheese, grated
20 small stuffed green olives
freshly snipped chives,
    to garnish
freshly cooked pasta,
    to serve

To make the tomato sauce, heat half the olive oil in a saucepan and cook half the chopped onion for 5 minutes, until softened. Add the garlic, chopped tomatoes, tomato paste, mixed herbs and red wine to the pan and season to taste with salt and pepper. Stir well until blended. Bring to the boil, then cover and simmer for 15 minutes.

To make the meatballs, place the pork, breadcrumbs, remaining onion, egg yolk and half the Parmesan in a large bowl. Season well and mix together with your hands. Divide the mixture into 20 balls.

Flatten 1 ball out in the palm of your hands, place an olive in the centre, then squeeze the meat around the olive to enclose completely. Repeat with remaining mixture and olives. Place the meatballs on a baking sheet and cover with clingfilm and chill in the refrigerator for 30 minutes.

Heat the remaining oil in a large frying pan and cook the meatballs for 8–10 minutes, turning occasionally, until golden brown. Pour in the sauce and heat through. Sprinkle with chives and the remaining Parmesan. Serve immediately with the freshly cooked pasta.

Italian Calf Liver

SERVES 6

450 g/1 lb calf liver, trimmed
1 onion, peeled and sliced
2 fresh bay leaves,
    coarsely torn
fresh parsley sprigs
fresh sage leaves
5 black peppercorns,
    lightly crushed
1 tbsp redcurrant

jelly, warmed
4 tbsp walnut or olive oil
4 tbsp red wine vinegar
3 tbsp plain white flour
salt and freshly ground
    black pepper
2 garlic cloves, peeled
    and crushed
1 red pepper, deseeded

and sliced
1 yellow pepper, deseeded
    and sliced
3 tbsp sun-dried tomatoes,
    chopped
150 ml/¼ pint chicken stock
fresh sage leaves, to garnish
diced sauté potatoes,
    to serve

Cut the liver into very thin slices and place in a shallow dish. Sprinkle over the onion, bay leaves, parsley, sage and peppercorns. Blend the redcurrant jelly with 1 tablespoon of the oil and the vinegar. Pour over the liver, cover and leave to marinate for at least 30 minutes.Turn the liver occasionally or spoon over the marinade.

Remove the liver from the marinade, strain the liquor and reserve. Season the flour with salt and pepper, then use to coat the liver. Add the remaining oil to a heavy based frying pan, then sauté the garlic and peppers for 5 minutes. Using a slotted spoon, remove from the pan.

Add the liver to the pan, turn the heat up to high and cook until the meat is browned on all sides. Return the garlic and peppers to the pan and add the reserved marinade, the sun-dried tomatoes and stock. Bring to the boil, then reduce the heat and simmer for 3–4 minutes, or until the liver is cooked. Add more seasoning, then garnish with a few sage leaves and serve immediately with diced sauté potatoes.

 Try this: FOR AN ALTERNATIVE: 194 FOR A LIGHT BITE: 52

Spaghetti Bolognese

SERVES 4

3 tbsp olive oil
50 g/2 oz unsmoked streaky
   bacon, rind removed
   and chopped
1 small onion, peeled
   and finely chopped
1 carrot, peeled and
   finely chopped

1 celery, trimmed and
   finely chopped
2 garlic cloves, peeled
   and crushed
1 bay leaf
500 g/1 lb 2 oz minced
   beef steak
400 g can chopped tomatoes

2 tbsp tomato paste
150 ml/¼ pint red wine
150 ml/¼ pint beef stock
salt and freshly gound
   black pepper
450 g/1 lb spaghetti
freshly grated Parmesan
   cheese, to serve

Heat the olive oil in a large heavy-based pan, add the bacon and cook for 5 minutes or until slightly coloured. Add the onion, carrot, celery, garlic and bay leaf and cook, stirring, for 8 minutes, or until the vegetables are soft.

Add the minced beef to the pan and cook, stirring with a wooden spoon to break up any lumps in the meat, for 5-8 minutes, or until browned.

Stir the tomatoes and tomato paste into the mince and pour in the wine and stock. Bring to the boil, lower the heat and simmer for a least 40 minutes, stirring occasionally. The longer you leave the sauce to cook, the more intense the flavour. Season to taste with salt and pepper and remove the bay leaf.

Meanwhile, bring a large pan of lightly salted water to a rolling boil, add the spaghetti and cook for about 8 minutes or until 'al dente'. Drain and arrange on warmed serving plates. Top with the prepared Bolognese sauce and serve immediately sprinkled with grated Parmesan cheese.

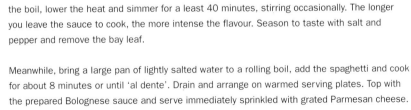

Try this: FOR AN ALTERNATIVE: 132   FOR A LIGHT BITE: 54

Spaghetti & Meatballs

SERVES 4

400 g can chopped tomatoes
1 tbsp tomato paste
1 tsp chilli sauce
1/4 tsp brown sugar
salt and freshly ground
    black pepper
350 g/12 oz spaghetti
75g/3 oz Cheddar cheese,
    grated, plus extra to serve

freshly chopped parsley,
    to garnish

For the meatballs:
450 g/1 lb lean pork or
    beef mince
125 g/4 oz fresh
    breadcrumbs
1 large onion, peeled and

finely chopped
1 medium egg, beaten
1 tbsp tomato paste
2 tbsp freshly chopped
    parsley
1 tbsp freshly chopped
    oregano

Preheat the oven to 200°C/400°F/Gas Mark 6, 15minutes before using. Place the chopped tomatoes, tomato paste, chilli sauce and sugar in a saucepan. Season to taste with salt and pepper and bring to the boil. Cover and simmer for 15 minutes, then cook, uncovered, for a further 10 minutes, or until the sauce has reduced and thickened.

Meanwhile, make the meatballs. Place the meat, breadcrumbs and onion in a food processor. Blend until all the ingredients are well mixed. Add the beaten egg, tomato paste, parsley and oregano and season to taste. Blend again.

Shape the mixture into small balls, about the size of an apricot, and place on an oiled baking tray. Cook in the preheated oven for 25–30 minutes, or until browned and cooked.

Meanwhile, bring a large pan of lightly salted water to a rolling boil. Add the pasta and cook according to the packet instructions, or until 'al dente'.

Drain the pasta and return to the pan. Pour over the tomato sauce and toss gently to coat the spaghetti. Tip into a warmed serving dish and top with the meatballs. Garnish with chopped parsley and serve immediately with grated cheese.

Try this: FOR AN ALTERNATIVE: 146   FOR A LIGHT BITE: 64

Chorizo with Pasta in a Tomato Sauce

SERVES 6

25 g/1 oz butter
2 tbsp olive oil
2 large onions, peeled and
　finely sliced
1 tsp soft brown sugar
2 garlic cloves, peeled
　and crushed

225 g/8 oz chorizo, sliced
1 chilli, deseeded and
　finely sliced
400g can chopped tomatoes
1 tbsp sun-dried
　tomato paste
150 ml/¼ pint red wine

salt and freshly ground
　black pepper
450 g/1 lb rigatoni
freshly chopped parsley,
　to garnish

Melt the butter with the olive oil in a large heavy-based pan. Add the onions and sugar and cook over a very low heat, stirring occasionally, for 15 minutes, or until soft and starting to caramelize.

Add the garlic and chorizo to the pan and cook for 5 minutes. Stir in the chilli, chopped tomatoes and tomato paste, and pour in the wine. Season well with salt and pepper. Bring to the boil, cover, reduce the heat and simmer for 30 minutes, stirring occasionally. Remove the lid and simmer for a further 10 minutes, or until the sauce starts to thicken.

Meanwhile, bring a large pan of lightly salted water to a rolling boil. Add the pasta and cook according to the packet instructions, or until 'al dente'.

Drain the pasta, reserving 2 tablespoons of the water, and return to the pan. Add the chorizo sauce with the reserved cooking water and toss gently until the pasta is evenly covered. Tip into a warmed serving dish, sprinkle with the parsley and serve immediately.

Try this: FOR AN ALTERNATIVE: 126 FOR A LIGHT BITE: 56

Moroccan Penne

SERVES 6

1 tbsp sunflower oil
1 red onion, peeled and
  chopped
2 cloves garlic, peeled
  and crushed
1 tbsp coriander seeds
¼ tsp cumin seeds

¼ tsp freshly grated nutmeg
450 g/1 lb lean lamb mince
1 aubergine, trimmed
  and diced
400 g can chopped tomatoes
300 ml/½ pint vegetable stock
125 g/4 oz ready-to-eat

apricots, chopped
12 black olives, pitted
salt and freshly ground
  black pepper
350 g/12 oz penne
1 tbsp toasted pine nuts,
  to garnish

Preheat the oven to 200°C/400°F/Gas Mark 6, 15 minutes before using. Heat the sunflower oil in a large flameproof casserole. Add the chopped onion and fry for 5 minutes, or until softened.

Using a pestle and mortar, pound the garlic, coriander seeds, cumin seeds and grated nutmeg together into a paste. Add to the onion and cook for 3 minutes.

Add the lamb mince to the casserole and fry, stirring with a wooden spoon, for 4–5 minutes, or until the mince has broken up and browned.

Add the aubergine to the mince and fry for 5 minutes. Stir in the chopped tomatoes and vegetable stock and bring to the boil. Add the apricots and olives, then season well with salt and pepper. Return to the boil, lower the heat and simmer for 15 minutes.

Add the penne to the casserole, stir well, then cover and place in the preheated oven. Cook for 10 minutes then stir and return to the oven, uncovered, for a further 15–20 minutes, or until the pasta is 'al dente'. Remove from the oven, sprinkle with toasted pine nuts and serve immediately.

Try this: FOR AN ALTERNATIVE: 170 FOR A LIGHT BITE: 22

Spicy Chilli Beef

SERVES 4

2 tbsp olive oil
1 onion, peeled and
   finely chopped
1 red pepper, deseeded
   and sliced
450 g/1 lb minced beef steak
2 garlic cloves, peeled
   and crushed

2 red chillies, deseeded
   and finely sliced
salt and freshly ground
   black pepper
400 g can chopped tomatoes
2 tbsp tomato paste
400 g can red kidney
   beans, drained

50 g/2 oz good quality, plain
   dark chocolate, grated
350 g/12 oz dried fusilli
knob of butter
2 tbsp freshly chopped
   flat-leaf parsley
paprika, to garnish
soured cream, to serve

Heat the olive oil in a large heavy-based pan. Add the onion and red pepper and cook for 5 minutes, or until beginning to soften. Add the minced beef and cook over a high heat for 5–8 minutes, or until the meat is browned. Stir with a wooden spoon during cooking to break up any lumps in the meat. Add the garlic and chilli, fry for 1 minute then season to taste with salt and pepper.

Add the chopped tomatoes, tomato paste and the kidney beans to the pan. Bring to the boil, lower the heat, and simmer, covered, for at least 40 minutes, stirring occasionally. Stir in the grated chocolate and cook for 3 minutes, or until melted.

Meanwhile, bring a large pan of lightly salted water to a rolling boil. Add the fusilli and cook according to the packet instructions, or until 'al dente'.

Drain the pasta, return to the pan and toss with the butter and parsley. Tip into a warmed serving dish or spoon on to individual plates. Spoon the sauce over the pasta. Sprinkle with paprika and serve immediately with spoonfuls of soured cream.

Try this: FOR AN ALTERNATIVE: 226 FOR A LIGHT BITE: 60

Pasta & Pork Ragù

SERVES 4

1 tbsp sunflower oil
1 leek, trimmed and
  thinly sliced
225 g/8 oz pork fillet, diced
1 garlic clove, peeled
  and crushed
2 tsp paprika

¼ tsp cayenne pepper
150 ml/½ pint white wine
600 ml/1 pint
  vegetable stock
400g can borlotti beans,
  drained and rinsed
2 carrots, peeled and diced

salt and freshly ground
  black pepper
225 g/8 oz fresh egg
  tagliatelle
1 tbsp freshly chopped
  parsley, to garnish
crème fraîche, to serve

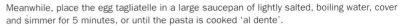

Heat the sunflower oil in a large frying pan. Add the sliced leek and cook, stirring frequently, for 5 minutes, or until softened. Add the pork and cook, stirring, for 4 minutes, or until sealed.

Add the crushed garlic and the paprika and cayenne peppers to the pan and stir until all the pork is lightly coated in the garlic and pepper mixture.

Pour in the wine and 450 ml/¾ pint of the vegetable stock. Add the borlotti beans and carrots and season to taste with salt and pepper. Bring the sauce to the boil, then lower the heat and simmer for 5 minutes.

Meanwhile, place the egg tagliatelle in a large saucepan of lightly salted, boiling water, cover and simmer for 5 minutes, or until the pasta is cooked 'al dente'.

Drain the pasta, then add to the pork ragù; toss well. Adjust the seasoning, then tip into a warmed serving dish. Sprinkle with chopped parsley and serve with a little crème fraîche.

Try this: FOR AN ALTERNATIVE: 164 FOR A LIGHT BITE: 36

Sausage & Redcurrant Pasta Bake

SERVES 4

450 g/1 lb good quality, thick pork sausages
2 tsp sunflower oil
25 g/1 oz butter
1 onion, peeled and sliced
2 tbsp plain white flour
450 ml/¾ pint chicken stock

150 ml/¼ pint port or good quality red wine
1 tbsp freshly chopped thyme leaves, plus sprigs to garnish
1 bay leaf
4 tbsp redcurrant jelly

salt and freshly ground black pepper
350 g/12 oz fresh penne
75 g/3 oz Gruyère cheese, grated

Preheat the oven to 220°C/425°F/Gas Mark 7, 15 minutes before cooking. Prick the sausages, place in a shallow ovenproof dish and toss in the sunflower oil. Cook in the oven for 25–30 minutes, or until golden brown.

Meanwhile, melt the butter in a frying pan, add the sliced onion and fry for 5 minutes, or until golden-brown. Stir in the flour and cook for 2 minutes. Remove the pan from the heat and gradually stir in the chicken stock with the port or red wine.

Return the pan to the heat and bring to the boil, stirring continuously until the sauce starts to thicken. Add the thyme, bay leaf and redcurrant jelly and season well with salt and pepper. Simmer the sauce for 5 minutes.

Bring a large pan of salted water to a rolling boil, add the pasta and cook for about 4 minutes, or until 'al dente'. Drain thoroughly and reserve.

Lower the oven temperature to 200°C/400°F/Gas Mark 6. Remove the sausages from the oven, drain off any excess fat and return the sausages to the dish. Add the pasta. Pour over the sauce, removing the bay leaf, and toss together. Sprinkle with the Gruyère cheese and return to the oven for 15–20 minutes, or until bubbling and golden-brown. Serve immediately, garnished with thyme sprigs.

Pappardelle Pork
with Brandy Sauce

SERVES 4

4 pork fillets, each weighing about 175 g/6 oz	pepper	350 g/12 oz pappardelle
1 tbsp freshly chopped sage, plus whole leaves to garnish	4 slices Parma ham	1–2 tsp butter
	1 tbsp olive oil	2 tbsp freshly chopped flat-leaf parsley
salt and freshly ground black	6 tbsp brandy	
	300 ml/½ pint chicken stock	
	200 ml/7 fl oz double cream	

Preheat the oven to 200°C/400°F/Gas Mark 6, 15 minutes before cooking. Using a sharp knife, cut two slits in each pork fillet then stuff each slit with chopped sage. Season well with salt and pepper and wrap each fillet with a slice of Parma ham.

Heat the olive oil in a large frying pan. Add the wrapped pork fillets and cook, turning once, for 1–2 minutes, or until the Parma ham is golden brown. Transfer to a roasting tin and cook in the preheated oven for 10–12 minutes.

Return the frying pan to the heat and add the brandy, scraping the bottom of the pan with a spoon to release all the flavours. Boil for 1 minute, then pour in the chicken stock. Boil for a further 2 minutes then pour in the cream and boil again for 2–3 minutes, or until the sauce has thickened slightly. Season the brandy sauce to taste.

Bring a large pan of lightly salted water to a rolling boil. Add the pasta and cook according to the packet instructions, or until 'al dente'. Drain the pasta thoroughly and return to the pan. Add the butter and chopped parsley and toss together. Keep the pasta warm.

Remove the pork from the oven and pour any juices into the brandy sauce. Pile the pasta on individual plates, season with pepper, spoon over the brandy sauce and serve immediately with the pork fillets.

Try this: FOR AN ALTERNATIVE: 160 FOR A LIGHT BITE: 60

Pasta with Beef, Capers & Olives

SERVES 4

2 tbsp olive oil
300 g/11 oz rump steak, trimmed and cut into strips
4 spring onions, trimmed and sliced
2 garlic cloves, peeled and chopped

2 courgettes, trimmed and cut into strips
1 red pepper, deseeded and cut into strips
2 tsp freshly chopped oregano
2 tbsp capers, drained and rinsed

4 tbsp pitted black olives, sliced
400 g can chopped tomatoes
salt and freshly ground black pepper
450 g/1 lb fettuccine
1 tbsp freshly chopped parsley, to garnish

Heat the olive oil in a large frying pan over a high heat. Add the steak and cook, stirring, for 3–4 minutes, or until browned. Remove from the pan using a slotted spoon and reserve.

Lower the heat, add the spring onions and garlic to the pan and cook for 1 minute. Add the courgettes and pepper and cook for 3–4 minutes.

Add the oregano, capers and olives to the pan with the chopped tomatoes. Season to taste with salt and pepper, then simmer for 7 minutes, stirring occasionally. Return the beef to the pan and simmer for 3–5 minutes, or until the sauce has thickened slightly.

Meanwhile, bring a large pan of lightly salted water to a rolling boil. Add the pasta and cook according to the packet instructions, or until 'al dente'.

Drain the pasta thoroughly. Return to the pan and add the beef sauce. Toss gently until the pasta is lightly coated. Tip into a warmed serving dish or on to individual plates. Sprinkle with chopped parsley and serve immediately.

Try this: FOR AN ALTERNATIVE: 134 FOR A LIGHT BITE: 32

Gnocchi & Parma Ham Bake

SERVES 4

3 tbsp olive oil
1 red onion, peeled
    and sliced
2 garlic cloves, peeled
175 g/6 oz plum tomatoes,
    skinned and quartered
2 tbsp sun-dried tomato paste

250 g tub mascarpone cheese
salt and freshly ground
    black pepper
1 tbsp freshly chopped
    tarragon
300 g/11 oz fresh gnocchi
125 g/4 oz Cheddar or

Parmesan cheese, grated
50 g/2 oz fresh white
    breadcrumbs
50 g/2 oz Parma ham, sliced
10 pitted green olives, halved
sprigs of flat-leaf parsley,
    to garnish

Heat the oven to 180°C/350°F/Gas Mark 4, 10 minutes before cooking. Heat 2 tablespoons of the olive oil in a large frying pan and cook the onion and garlic for 5 minutes, or until softened. Stir in the tomatoes, sun-dried tomato paste and mascarpone cheese. Season to taste with salt and pepper. Add half the tarragon. Bring to the boil, then lower the heat immediately and simmer for 5 minutes.

Meanwhile, bring 1.7 litres/3 pints water to the boil in a large pan. Add the remaining olive oil and a good pinch of salt. Add the gnocchi and cook for 1–2 minutes, or until they rise to the surface.

Drain the gnocchi thoroughly and transfer to a large ovenproof dish. Add the tomato sauce and toss gently to coat the pasta. Combine the Cheddar or Parmesan cheese with the breadcrumbs and remaining tarragon and scatter over the pasta mixture. Top with the Parma ham and olives and season again.

Cook in the preheated oven for 20–25 minutes, or until golden and bubbling. Serve immediately, garnished with parsley sprigs.

Lamb Arrabbiata

SERVES 4

4 tbsp olive oil
450 g/1 lb lamb fillets, cubed
1 large onion, peeled and
  sliced
4 garlic cloves, peeled and
  finely chopped
1 red chilli, deseeded and
  finely chopped
400 g can chopped tomatoes
175 g/6 oz pitted black
  olives, halved
150 ml/¼ pint white wine
salt and freshly ground
  black pepper
275 g/10 oz farfalle pasta
1 tsp butter
4 tbsp freshly chopped
  parsley, plus1 tbsp
  to garnish

Heat 2 tablespoons of the olive oil in a large frying pan and cook the lamb for 5–7 minutes, or until sealed. Remove from the pan using a slotted spoon and reserve.

Heat the remaining oil in the pan, add the onion, garlic and chilli and cook until softened. Add the tomatoes, bring to the boil, then simmer for 10 minutes.

Return the browned lamb to the pan with the olives and pour in the wine. Bring the sauce back to the boil, reduce the heat then simmer, uncovered, for 15 minutes, until the lamb is tender. Season to taste with salt and pepper.

Meanwhile, bring a large pan of lightly salted water to a rolling boil. Add the pasta and cook according to the packet instructions, or until 'al dente'.

Drain the pasta, toss in the butter, then add to the sauce and mix lightly. Stir in 4 tablespoons of the chopped parsley, then tip into a warmed serving dish. Sprinkle with the remaining parsley and serve immediately.

Try this: FOR AN ALTERNATIVE: 86 FOR A LIGHT BITE: 22

Creamed Lamb & Wild Mushroom Pasta

SERVES 6

25 g/1 oz dried porcini
450 g/1 lb pasta shapes
25g/1 oz butter
1 tbsp olive oil
350 g/12 oz lamb neck
  fillet, thinly sliced
1 garlic clove, peeled

and crushed
225 g/8 oz brown or wild
  mushrooms, wiped
  and sliced
4 tbsp white wine
125 ml/4 fl oz double cream
salt and freshly ground

black pepper
1 tbsp freshly chopped
  parsley, to garnish
freshly grated Parmesan
  cheese, to serve

Place the porcini in a small bowl and cover with almost boiling water. Leave to soak for 30 minutes. Drain the porcini, reserving the soaking liquid. Chop the porcini finely.

Bring a large pan of lightly salted water to a rolling boil. Add the pasta and cook according to the packet instructions, or until 'al dente'.

Meanwhile, melt the butter with the olive oil in a large frying pan and fry the lamb to seal. Add the garlic, mushrooms and prepared porcini and cook for 5 minutes, or until just soft.

Add the wine and the reserved porcini soaking liquid, then simmer for 2 minutes. Stir in the cream with the sesasoning and simmer for 1–2 minutes, or until just thickened.

Drain the pasta thoroughly, reserving about 4 tablespoons of the cooking water. Return the pasta to the pan. Pour over the mushroom sauce and toss lightly together, adding the pasta water if the sauce is too thick. Tip into a warmed serving dish or spoon on to individual plates. Garnish with the chopped parsley and serve immediately with grated Parmesan cheese.

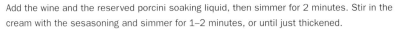

Try this: FOR AN ALTERNATIVE: 130 FOR A LIGHT BITE: 64

Tagliatelle with Creamy Liver & Basil

SERVES 4

25 g/1 oz plain flour
salt and freshly ground
  black pepper
450 g/1 lb lamb's liver, thinly
  sliced and cut into
  bite-sized pieces
25 g/1 oz butter

1 tbsp olive oil
2 red onions, peeled
  and sliced
1 garlic clove, peeled
  and sliced
150 ml/¼ pint chicken stock
1 tbsp tomato paste

2 sun-dried tomatoes,
  finely chopped
1 tbsp freshly chopped basil
150 ml/¼ pint double cream
350 g/12 oz tagliatelle verdi
fresh basil leaves, to garnish

Season the flour lightly with salt and pepper and place in a large plastic bag. Add the liver and toss gently to coat. Remove the liver from the bag and reserve.

Melt the butter with the olive oil in a large frying pan. Add the onion and garlic and fry for 6–8 minutes, or until the onions begin to colour. Add the liver and fry until brown on all sides.

Stir in the chicken stock, tomato paste and sun-dried tomatoes. Bring to the boil, reduce the heat and simmer very gently for 10 minutes.

Meanwhile, bring a large pan of lightly salted water to a rolling boil. Add the pasta and cook according to the packet instructions, or until 'al dente'.

Stir the chopped basil and cream into the liver sauce and season to taste.

Drain the pasta thoroughly, reserving 2 tablespoons of the cooking water. Tip the pasta into a warmed serving dish or pile on to individual plates. Stir the reserved cooking water into the liver sauce and pour over the pasta. Toss lightly to coat the pasta. Garnish with basil leaves and serve immediately.

 Try this: FOR AN ALTERNATIVE: 148   FOR A LIGHT BITE: 52

Gammon with Red Wine Sauce & Pasta

SERVES 4

25 g/1 oz butter	1 tsp soft brown sugar	3 tbsp wholegrain mustard
150 ml/¼ pint red wine	225 g/8 oz gammon steak,	2 tbsp freshly chopped
4 red onions, peeled	trimmed	flat-leaf parsley, plus
and sliced	freshly ground black pepper	sprigs to garnish
4 tbsp orange juice	175 g/6 oz fusilli	

Preheat the grill to a medium heat before cooking. Heat the butter with the red wine in a large heavy-based pan. Add the onions, cover with a tight fitting lid and cook over a very low heat for 30 minutes, or until softened and transparent. Remove the lid from the pan, stir in the orange juice and sugar, then increase the heat and cook for about 10 minutes, until the onions are golden.

Meanwhile cook the gammon steak under the preheated grill, turning at least once, for 4–6 minutes, or until tender. Cut the cooked gammon into bite-sized pieces. Reserve and keep warm.

Meanwhile, bring a large pan of very lightly salted water to a rolling boil. Add the pasta and cook according to the packet instructions, or until 'al dente'. Drain the pasta thoroughly, return to the pan, season with a little pepper and keep warm.

Stir the wholegrain mustard and chopped parsley into the onion sauce then pour over the pasta. Add the gammon pieces to the pan and toss lightly to thoroughly coat the pasta with the sauce. Pile the pasta mixture on to 2 warmed serving plates. Garnish with sprigs of flat-leaf parsley and serve immediately.

Gnocchi with Tuscan Beef Ragù

SERVES 4

25 g/1 oz dried porcini
3 tbsp olive oil
1 small onion, peeled and
   finely chopped
1 carrot, peeled and
   finely chopped
1 celery, trimmed and
   finely chopped
1 fennel bulb, trimmed
and sliced
2 garlic cloves, peeled
   and crushed
450 g/1 lb fresh beef
   steak mince
4 tbsp red wine
50 g/2 oz pine nuts
1 tbsp freshly chopped
   rosemary
2 tbsp tomato paste
400 g can chopped tomatoes
225 g/8 oz fresh gnocchi
salt and freshly ground
   black pepper
100 g/4 oz mozzarella
   cheese, cubed

Preheat the oven to 200°C/400°F/Gas Mark 6, 15 minutes before cooking. Place the porcini in a small bowl and cover with almost boiling water. Leave to soak for 30 minutes. Drain, reserving the soaking liquid and straining it through a muslin-lined sieve. Chop the porcini.

Heat the olive oil in a large heavy-based pan. Add the onion, carrot, celery, fennel and garlic and cook for 8 minutes, stirring, or until soft. Add the minced steak and cook, stirring, for 5–8 minutes, or until sealed and any lumps are broken up.

Pour in the wine, then add the porcini with half the pine nuts, the rosemary and tomato paste. Stir in the porcini soaking liquid then simmer for 5 minutes. Add the chopped tomatoes and simmer gently for about 40 minutes, stirring occasionally.

Meanwhile, bring 1.7 litres/3 pints of lightly salted water to a rolling boil in a large pan. Add the gnocchi and cook for 1–2 minutes, until they rise to the surface.

Drain the gnocchi and place in an ovenproof dish. Stir in three-quarters of the mozzarella cheese with the beef sauce. Top with the remaining mozzarella and pine nuts, then bake in the preheated oven for 20 minutes, until golden-brown. Serve immediately.

Try this: FOR AN ALTERNATIVE: 160   FOR A LIGHT BITE: 18

Poultry & Game

Saffron Roast Chicken with Crispy Onions

SERVES 4-6

1.6 kg/3½ lb oven-ready chicken, preferably free range
75 g/3 oz butter, softened
1 tsp saffron strands, lightly toasted
grated rind of 1 lemon

2 tbsp freshly chopped flat-leaf parsley
2 tbsp extra-virgin olive oil
450 g/1 lb onions, peeled and cut into thin wedges
8–12 garlic cloves, peeled
1 tsp cumin seeds

½ tsp ground cinnamon
50 g/2 oz pine nuts
50 g/2 oz sultanas
salt and freshly ground black pepper
sprig of fresh flat-leaf parsley, to garnish

Preheat oven to 200°C/400°F/Gas Mark 6. Using your fingertips, gently loosen the skin from the chicken breast by sliding your hand between the skin and flesh. Cream together 50 g/2 oz of the butter with the saffron threads, the lemon rind and half the parsley, until smooth. Push the butter under the skin. Spread over the breast and the top of the thighs with your fingers. Pull the neck skin to tighten the skin over the breast and tuck under the bird, then secure with a skewer or cocktail stick.

Heat the olive oil and remaining butter in a large heavy-based frying pan and cook the onions and garlic cloves for 5 minutes, or until the onions are soft. Stir in the cumin seeds, cinnamon, pine nuts and sultanas and cook for 2 minutes. Season to taste with salt and pepper and place in a roasting tin.

Place the chicken, breast-side down, on the base of the onions and roast in the preheated oven for 45 minutes. Reduce the oven temperature to 170°C/325°F/Gas Mark 3. Turn the chicken breast-side up and stir the onions. Continue roasting until the chicken is a deep golden yellow and the onions are crisp. Allow to rest for 10 minutes, then sprinkle with the remaining parsley. Before serving, garnish with a sprig of parsley and serve immediately with the onions and garlic.

Try this: FOR AN ALTERNATIVE: 188 FOR A LIGHT BITE: 24

Pheasant with Sage & Blueberries

SERVES 4

3 tbsp olive oil	salt and freshly ground	dry white wine
3 shallots, peeled and	black pepper	200 ml/⅓ pint chicken stock
coarsely chopped	2 pheasants or guinea fowl,	3 tbsp double cream or
2 sprigs of fresh sage,	rinsed and dried	butter (optional)
coarsely chopped	125 g/4 oz blueberries	1 tbsp brandy
1 bay leaf	4 slices Parma ham or bacon	roast potatoes, to serve
1 lemon, halved	125 ml/4 fl oz vermouth or	

Preheat oven to 180°C/350°F/Gas Mark 4, 10 minutes before cooking. Place the oil, shallots, sage and bay leaf in a bowl, with the juice from the lemon halves. Season with salt and pepper. Tuck each of the squeezed lemon halves into the birds with 75 g/3 oz of the blueberries, then rub the birds with the marinade and leave for 2–3 hours, basting occasionally.

Remove the birds from the marinade and cover each with 2 slices of Parma ham. Tie the legs of each bird with string and place in a roasting tin. Pour over the marinade and add the vermouth. Roast in the preheated oven for 1 hour, or until tender and golden and the juices run clear when a thigh is pierced with a sharp knife or skewer.

Transfer to a warm serving plate, cover with tinfoil and discard the string. Skim off any surface fat from the tin and set over a medium-high heat. Add the stock to the tin and bring to the boil, scraping any browned bits from the bottom. Boil until slightly reduced. Whisk in the cream or butter, if using, and simmer until thickened, whisking constantly. Stir in the brandy and strain into a gravy jug. Add the remaining blueberries and keep warm.

Using a sharp carving knife, cut each of the birds in half and arrange on the plate with the crispy Parma ham. Serve immediately with roast potatoes and the gravy.

Try this: FOR AN ALTERNATIVE: 206 FOR A LIGHT BITE: 44

Chicken Cacciatore

SERVES 4

2–3 tbsp olive oil
125 g/4 oz pancetta or
    streaky bacon, diced
25 g/1 oz plain flour
salt and freshly ground
    black pepper
1.4–1.6 kg/3–3½ lb chicken,
    cut into 8 pieces
2 garlic cloves, peeled

and chopped
125 ml/4 fl oz red wine
400 g can chopped tomatoes
150 ml/¼ pint chicken stock
12 small onions, peeled
1 bay leaf
1 tsp brown sugar
1 tsp dried oregano
1 green pepper, deseeded

and chopped
225 g/8 oz chestnut or field
    mushrooms, thickly sliced
2 tbsp freshly chopped
    parsley
freshly cooked tagliatelle,
    to serve

Heat 1 tablespoon of the olive oil in a large, deep frying pan and add the diced pancetta or bacon and stir-fry for 2–3 minutes, or until crisp and golden brown. Using a slotted spoon, transfer the pancetta or bacon to a plate and reserve.

Season the flour with salt and pepper, then use to coat the chicken. Heat the remaining oil in the pan and brown the chicken pieces on all sides for about 15 minutes. Remove from the pan and add to the bacon.

Stir the garlic into the pan and cook for about 30 seconds. Add the red wine and cook, stirring and scraping any browned bits from the base of the pan. Allow the wine to boil until it is reduced by half. Add the tomatoes, stock, onions, bay leaf, brown sugar and oregano and stir well. Season to taste.

Return the chicken and bacon to the pan and bring to the boil. Cover and simmer for 30 minutes, then stir in the peppers and mushrooms and simmer for a further 15–20 minutes, or until the chicken and vegetables are tender and the sauce is reduced and slightly thickened. Stir in the chopped parsley and serve immediately with freshly cooked tagliatelle.

Try this: FOR AN ALTERNATIVE: 216 FOR A LIGHT BITE: 60

Lemon Chicken with Potatoes, Rosemary & Olives

SERVES 6

12 skinless boneless
  chicken thighs
1 large lemon
125 ml/4 fl oz extra-virgin
  olive oil
6 garlic cloves, peeled
  and sliced

2 onions, peeled and
  thinly sliced
bunch of fresh rosemary
1.1 kg/2½ lb potatoes,
  peeled and cut into 4
  cm/1½ inch pieces
salt and freshly ground

  black pepper
18–24 black olives, pitted
steamed carrots, to serve
courgettes, to serve

Preheat oven to 200°C/400°F/Gas Mark 6, 15 minutes before cooking. Trim the chicken thighs and place in a shallow baking dish large enough to hold them in a single layer. Remove the rind from the lemon with a zester or if using a peeler cut into thin julienne strips. Reserve half and add the remainder to the chicken. Squeeze the lemon juice over the chicken, toss to coat well and leave to stand for 10 minutes.

Transfer the chicken to a roasting tin. Add the remaining lemon zest or julienne strips, olive oil, garlic, onions and half of the rosemary sprigs. Toss gently and leave for about 20 minutes.

Cover the potatoes with lightly salted water and bring to the boil. Cook for 2 minutes, then drain well and add to the chicken. Season to taste with salt and pepper.

Roast the chicken in the preheated oven for 50 minutes, turning frequently and basting, or until the chicken is cooked. Just before the end of cooking time, discard the rosemary, and add fresh sprigs of rosemary. Add the olives and stir. Serve immediately with steamed carrots and courgettes.

Try this: FOR AN ALTERNATIVE: 182   FOR A LIGHT BITE: 38

Chicken with Porcini Mushrooms & Cream

SERVES 4

2 tbsp olive oil
4 boneless chicken breasts,
   preferably free range
2 garlic cloves, peeled
   and crushed
150 ml/¼ pint dry vermouth

or dry white wine
salt and freshly ground
   black pepper
25 g/1 oz butter
450 g/1 lb porcini or wild
   mushrooms, thickly sliced

1 tbsp freshly chopped
   oregano
sprigs of fresh basil,
   to garnish (optional)
freshly cooked rice, to serve

Heat the olive oil in a large, heavy-based frying pan, then add the chicken breasts, skin-side down and cook for about 10 minutes, or until they are well browned. Remove the chicken breasts and reserve. Add the garlic, stir into the juices and cook for 1 minute.

Pour the vermouth or white wine into the pan and season to taste with salt and pepper. Return the chicken to the pan. Bring to the boil, reduce the heat to low and simmer for about 20 minutes, or until tender.

In another large frying pan, heat the butter and add the sliced porcini or wild mushrooms. Stir-fry for about 5 minutes, or until the mushrooms are golden and tender.

Add the porcini or wild mushrooms and any juices to the chicken. Season to taste, then add the chopped oregano. Stir together gently and cook for 1 minute longer. Transfer to a large serving plate and garnish with sprigs of fresh basil, if desired. Serve immediately with rice.

Try this: FOR AN ALTERNATIVE: 130 FOR A LIGHT BITE: 64

Turkey Escalopes Marsala with Wilted Watercress

SERVES 4

4 turkey escalopes, each about 150 g/5 oz	black pepper	wiped and quartered
25 g/1 oz plain flour	1–2 tbsp olive oil	50 ml/2 fl oz dry Marsala
½ tsp dried thyme	125 g/4 oz watercress	wine
salt and freshly ground	40 g/1½ oz butter	50 ml/2 fl oz chicken stock
	225 g/8 oz mushrooms,	or water

Place each turkey escalope between 2 sheets of non-stick baking parchment and using a meat mallet or rolling pin pound to make an escalope about 3 mm/⅛ inch thick. Put the flour in a shallow dish, add the thyme, season to taste with salt and pepper and stir to blend. Coat each escalope lightly on both sides with the flour mixture, then reserve.

Heat the olive oil in a large frying pan, then add the watercress and stir-fry for about 2 minutes, until just wilted and brightly coloured. Season with salt and pepper. Using a slotted spoon, transfer the watercress to a plate and keep warm.

Add half the butter to the frying pan and when melted, add the mushrooms. Stir-fry for 4 minutes, or until golden and tender. Remove from the pan and reserve.

Add the remaining butter to the pan and, working in batches if necessary, cook the flour-coated escalopes for 2–3 minutes on each side, or until golden and cooked thoroughly, adding the remaining oil, if necessary. Remove from the pan and keep warm.

Add the Marsala wine to the pan and stir, scraping up any browned bits from the bottom of the pan. Add the stock or water and bring to the boil over a high heat. Season lightly. Return the escalopes and mushrooms to the pan and reheat gently until piping hot. Divide the warm watercress between 4 serving plates. Arrange 1 escalope over each serving of wilted watercress and spoon over the mushrooms and Marsala sauce. Serve immediately.

Try this: FOR AN ALTERNATIVE: 224   FOR A LIGHT BITE: 48

Chicken Liver & Tomato Sauce with Tagliolini

SERVES 4

50 ml/2 fl oz extra-virgin olive oil

1 onion, peeled and finely chopped

2 garlic cloves, peeled and finely chopped

125 ml/4 fl oz dry red wine

2 x 400 g cans Italian peeled

plum tomatoes with juice

1 tbsp tomato purée

1 tbsp freshly chopped sage or thyme leaves

salt and freshly ground black pepper

350 g/12 oz fresh or dried tagliolini, papardelle or

tagliatelle

25 g/1 oz butter

225 g/8 oz fresh chicken livers, trimmed and cut in half

plain flour for dusting

sprigs of fresh sage, to garnish (optional)

Heat half the olive oil in a large, deep, heavy-based frying pan and add the onion. Cook, stirring frequently, for 4–5 minutes, or until soft and translucent. Stir in the garlic and cook for a further minute.

Add the red wine and cook, stirring until the wine is reduced by half, then add the tomatoes, tomato purée and half the sage or thyme. Bring to the boil, stirring to break up the tomatoes. Simmer for 30 minutes, stirring occasionally, or until the sauce has reduced and thickened. Season to taste with salt and pepper. Bring a large saucepan of lightly salted water to the boil. Add the pasta and cook for 7–10 minutes, or until 'al dente'.

Meanwhile, in a large heavy-based frying pan, melt the remaining oil and the butter and heat until very hot. Pat the chicken livers dry and dust lightly with a little flour. Add to the pan, a few at a time, and cook for 5 minutes, or until crisp and browned, turning carefully – the livers should still be pink inside.

Drain the pasta well and turn into a large, warmed serving bowl. Stir the livers carefully into the tomato sauce, then pour the sauce over the drained pasta and toss gently to coat. Garnish with a sprig of fresh sage and serve immediately.

Try this: FOR AN ALTERNATIVE: 148   FOR A LIGHT BITE: 36

Creamy Chicken Cannelloni

SERVES 6

50 g/2 oz butter
2 garlic cloves, peeled and
    finely crushed
225 g/8 oz button
    mushrooms, thinly sliced
2 tbsp freshly chopped basil
450 g/1 lb fresh spinach,
    blanched
salt and freshly ground

black pepper
2 tbsp plain flour
300 ml/½ pint chicken stock
150 ml/¼ pint dry white wine
150 ml/¼ pint double cream
350 g/12 oz skinless,
    boneless, cooked
    chicken, chopped
175 g/6 oz Parma ham,

finely chopped
½ tsp dried thyme
225 g/8 oz precooked
    cannelloni tubes
175 g/6 oz Gruyère
    cheese, grated
40 g/1½ oz Parmesan
    cheese, grated
sprig of fresh basil, to garnish

Preheat oven to 190˚C/375˚F/Gas Mark 5, 10 minutes before cooking. Lightly butter a 28 x 23 cm/11 x 9 inch ovenproof baking dish. Heat half the butter in a large heavy-based frying pan, then add the garlic and mushrooms and cook gently for 5 minutes. Stir in the basil and the spinach and cook, covered, until the spinach is wilted and just tender, stirring frequently. Season to taste with salt and pepper, then spoon into the dish and reserve.

Melt the remaining butter in a small saucepan, then stir in the flour and cook for about 2 minutes, stirring constantly. Remove from the heat, stir in the stock, then the wine and the cream. Return to the heat, bring to the boil and simmer until thick and smooth, then season to taste.

Measure 125 ml/4 fl oz of the cream sauce into a bowl. Add the chopped chicken, Parma ham and the dried thyme. Season to taste, then spoon the chicken mixture into the cannelloni tubes, arranging them in 2 long rows on top of the spinach layer.

Add half the Gruyère cheese to the cream sauce and heat, stirring, until the cheese melts. Pour over the sauce and top with the remaining Gruyère and the Parmesan cheeses. Bake in the preheated oven for 35 minutes, or until golden and bubbling. Garnish with a sprig of fresh basil and serve immediately.

Try this: FOR AN ALTERNATIVE: 140 FOR A LIGHT BITE: 50

Duck Lasagna with Porcini & Basil

SERVES 6

1.4–1.8 kg/3–4 lb duck,
  quartered
1 onion, unpeeled and
  quartered
2 carrots, peeled and cut
  into pieces
1 celery stalk, cut into pieces
1 leek, trimmed and cut

into pieces
2 garlic cloves, unpeeled
  and smashed
1 tbsp black peppercorns
2 bay leaves
6–8 sprigs of fresh thyme
50 g/2 oz dried porcini
  mushrooms

125 ml/4 oz dry sherry
75 g/3 oz butter, diced
1 bunch of fresh basil leaves,
  stripped from stems
24 precooked lasagna sheets
75 g/3 oz Parmesan, grated
sprig of parsley, to garnish
mixed salad, to serve

Preheat oven to 180°C/350°F/Gas Mark 4, 10 minutes before cooking. Put the duck with the vegetables, garlic, peppercorns, bay leaves and thyme into a large stock pot and cover with cold water. Bring to the boil, skimming off any fat, then reduce the heat and simmer for 1 hour. Transfer the duck to a bowl and cool slightly. When cool enough to handle, remove the meat from the duck and dice. Return all the bones and trimmings to the simmering stock and continue to simmer for 1 hour. Strain the stock into a large bowl and leave until cold. Remove and discard the fat that has risen to the top.

Put the porcini in a colander and rinse under cold running water. Leave for 1 minute to dry off, then turn out on to a chopping board and chop finely. Place in a small bowl, then pour over the sherry and leave for about 1 hour, or until the porcini are plump and all the sherry is absorbed. Heat 25 g/1 oz of the butter in a frying pan. Shred the basil leaves and add to the hot butter, stirring until wilted. Add the soaked porcini and any liquid, mix well and reserve.

Oil a 30.5 x 23 cm/12 x 9 inch deep baking dish and pour a little stock into the base. Cover with 6–8 lasagna sheets, making sure that sheets slightly overlap. Continue to layer the pasta with a little stock, duck meat, the mushroom-basil mixture and Parmesan. Add a little butter every other layer. Cover with tinfoil and bake in the preheated oven for 40–45 minutes, or until cooked. Stand for 10 minutes before serving. Garnish with a sprig of parsley and serve with salad.

Try this: FOR AN ALTERNATIVE: 136   FOR A LIGHT BITE: 30

Turkey Tetrazzini

SERVES 4

275 g/10 oz green and
   white tagliatelle
50 g/2 oz butter
4 slices streaky bacon, diced
1 onion, peeled and
   finely chopped
175 g/6 oz mushrooms,
   thinly sliced
40 g/1½ oz plain flour

450 ml/¾ pint chicken stock
150 ml/¼ pint double cream
2 tbsp sherry
450 g/1 lb cooked
   turkey meat, cut into
   bite-sized pieces
1 tbsp freshly chopped
   parsley
freshly grated nutmeg

salt and freshly ground
   black pepper
25 g/1 oz Parmesan cheese,
   grated
freshly chopped parsley,
   to garnish
Parmesan cheese, grated,
   to garnish

Preheat oven to 180°C/350°F/Gas Mark 4. Lightly oil a large ovenproof dish. Bring a large saucepan of lightly salted water to the boil. Add the tagliatelle and cook for 7–9 minutes, or until 'al dente'. Drain well and reserve.

In a heavy-based saucepan, heat the butter and add the bacon. Cook for 2–3 minutes, or until crisp and golden. Add the onion and mushrooms and cook for 3–4 minutes, or until the vegetables are tender.

Stir in the flour and cook for 2 minutes. Remove from the heat and slowly stir in the stock. Return to the heat and cook, stirring until a smooth, thick sauce has formed. Add the tagliatelle, then pour in the cream and sherry. Add the turkey and parsley. Season to taste with the nutmeg and salt and pepper. Toss well to coat.

Turn the mixture into the prepared dish, spreading evenly. Sprinkle the top with the Parmesan cheese and bake in the preheated oven for 30–35 minutes, or until crisp, golden and bubbling. Garnish with chopped parsley and Parmesan cheese. Serve straight from the dish.

Try this: FOR AN ALTERNATIVE: 298   FOR A LIGHT BITE: 52

Poached Chicken with Salsa Verde Herb Sauce

SERVES 6

6 boneless chicken breasts, each about 175 g /6 oz
600 ml/1 pint chicken stock, preferably homemade

For the salsa verde:
2 garlic cloves, peeled and chopped
4 tbsp freshly chopped parsley

3 tbsp freshly chopped mint
2 tsp capers
2 tbsp chopped gherkins (optional)
2–3 anchovy fillets in olive oil, drained and finely chopped (optional)
1 handful wild rocket leaves, chopped (optional)
2 tbsp lemon juice or red

wine vinegar
125 ml/4 fl oz extra-virgin olive oil
salt and freshly ground black pepper
sprigs of mint, to garnish
freshly cooked vegetables, to serve

Place the chicken breasts with the stock in a large frying pan and bring to the boil. Reduce the heat and simmer for 10–15 minutes, or until cooked. Leave to cool in the stock.

To make the salsa verde, switch the motor on a food processor, then drop in the garlic cloves and chop finely. Add the parsley and mint and, using the pulse button, pulse 2–3 times. Add the capers and, if using, add the gherkins, anchovies and rocket. Pulse 2–3 times until the sauce is evenly textured.

With the machine still running, pour in the lemon juice or red wine vinegar, then add the olive oil in a slow, steady stream until the sauce is smooth. Season to taste with salt and pepper, then transfer to a large serving bowl and reserve.

Carve each chicken breast into thick slices and arrange on serving plates, fanning out the slices slightly. Spoon over a little of the salsa verde on to each chicken breast, garnish with sprigs of mint and serve immediately with freshly cooked vegetables.

Try this: FOR AN ALTERNATIVE: 208 FOR A LIGHT BITE: 20

Chicken & Asparagus with Tagliatelle

SERVES 4

275 g/10 oz fresh asparagus
50 g/2 oz butter
4 spring onions, trimmed
 and coarsely chopped
350 g/12 oz boneless,
 skinless chicken breast,

thinly sliced
2 tbsp white vermouth
300 ml/½ pint double cream
2 tbsp freshly chopped
 chives
400 g/14 oz fresh tagliatelle

50 g/2 oz Parmesan or
 pecorino cheese, grated
snipped chives, to garnish
extra Parmesan cheese
 (optional), to serve

Using a swivel-bladed vegetable peeler, lightly peel the asparagus stalks and then cook in lightly salted, boiling water for 2–3 minutes, or until just tender. Drain and refresh in cold water, then cut into 4 cm/1½ inch pieces and reserve.

Melt the butter in a large frying pan then add the spring onions and the chicken and fry for 4 minutes. Add the vermouth and allow to reduce until the liquid has evaporated. Pour in the cream and half the chives. Cook gently for 5–7 minutes, until the sauce has thickened and slightly reduced and the chicken is tender.

Bring a large saucepan of lightly salted water to the boil and cook the tagliatelle for 4–5 minutes, or until 'al dente'. Drain and immediately add to the chicken and cream sauce.

Using a pair of spaghetti tongs or kitchen forks, lightly toss the sauce and pasta until it is mixed thoroughly. Add the remaining chives and the Parmesan cheese and toss gently. Garnish with snipped chives and serve immediately, with extra Parmesan cheese, if you like.

Try this: FOR AN ALTERNATIVE: 220 FOR A LIGHT BITE: 52

Marinated Pheasant Breasts with Grilled Polenta

SERVES 4

3 tbsp extra-virgin olive oil
1 tbsp freshly chopped
    rosemary or sage leaves
½ tsp ground cinnamon
grated zest of 1 orange
salt and freshly ground
    black pepper

8 pheasant or wood
    pigeon breasts
600 ml/1 pint water
125 g/4 oz quick-cook
    polenta
2 tbsp butter, diced
40 g/1½ oz Parmesan

cheese, grated
1–2 tbsp freshly chopped
    parsley
assorted salad leaves,
    to serve

Preheat grill just before cooking. Blend 2 tablespoons of the olive oil with the chopped rosemary or sage, cinnamon and orange zest and season to taste with salt and pepper. Place the pheasant breasts in a large, shallow dish, pour over the oil and marinate until required, turning occasionally.

Bring the water and 1 teaspoon of salt to the boil in a large, heavy-based saucepan. Slowly whisk in the polenta in a thin, steady stream. Reduce the heat and simmer for 5–10 minutes, or until very thick, stirring constantly.

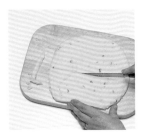

Stir the butter and cheese into the polenta, the parsley and a little black pepper. Turn the polenta out on to a lightly oiled, non-stick baking tray and spread into an even layer about 2 cm/¾ inch thick. Leave to cool, then chill in the refrigerator for about 1 hour.

Turn the cold polenta on to a work surface. Cut into 10 cm/4 inch squares. Brush with olive oil and arrange on a grill rack. Grill for 2–3 minutes on each side until crisp and golden, then cut each square into triangles and keep warm.

Transfer the marinated pheasant breasts to the grill and grill for 5 minutes, or until crisp and beginning to colour, turning once. Serve the pheasants immediately with the polenta and salad.

Try this: FOR AN ALTERNATIVE: 240   FOR A LIGHT BITE: 28

Braised Rabbit with Red Peppers

SERVES 4

1.1 kg/2½ lb rabbit pieces
125 ml/4 fl oz olive oil
grated zest and juice of
　1 lemon
2–3 tbsp freshly chopped
　thyme
salt and freshly ground

black pepper
1 onion, peeled and thinly
　sliced
4 red peppers, deseeded
　and cut into 2.5 cm/
　1 inch pieces
2 garlic cloves, peeled

and crushed
400 g can strained, crushed
　tomatoes
1 tsp brown sugar
freshly cooked polenta or
　creamy mashed potatoes,
　to serve

Place the rabbit pieces in a shallow dish with half the olive oil, the lemon zest and juice, thyme, and some black pepper. Turn until well coated, then cover and leave to marinate for about 1 hour.

Heat half the remaining oil in a large, heavy-based casserole dish, add the onion and cook for 5 minutes, then add the peppers and cook for a further 12–15 minutes, or until softened, stirring occasionally. Stir in the garlic, crushed tomatoes and brown sugar and cook, covered, until soft, stirring occasionally.

Heat the remaining oil in a large frying pan, drain the rabbit, reserving the marinade, and pat the rabbit dry with absorbent kitchen paper. Add the rabbit to the pan and cook on all sides until golden. Transfer the rabbit to the casserole dish and mix to cover with the tomato sauce.

Add the reserved marinade to the frying pan, cook stirring to loosen any browned bits from the pan, add to the rabbit and stir gently.

Cover the pan and simmer for 30 minutes or until the rabbit is tender. Serve the rabbit and the vegetable mixture on a bed of polenta or creamy mashed potatoes.

Try this: FOR AN ALTERNATIVE: 202 FOR A LIGHT BITE: 22

Hot Duck Pasta Salad

SERVES 6

3 boneless and skinless
  duck breasts
1 tbsp wholegrain mustard
1 tbsp clear honey
salt and freshly ground
  black pepper
4 medium eggs

450 g/1 lb fusilli
125 g/4 oz French beans,
  trimmed
1 large carrot, peeled and
  cut into thin batons
125 g/4 oz sweetcorn
  kernels, cooked if frozen

75 g/3 oz fresh baby spinach
  leaves, shredded

For the dresssing:
8 tbsp French dressing
1 tsp horseradish sauce
4 tbsp crème fraîche

Preheat the oven to 200°C/400°F/Gas Mark 6. Place the duck breasts on a baking tray lined with tinfoil. Mix together the wholegrain mustard and honey, season lightly with salt and pepper then spread over the duck breasts. Roast in the preheated oven for 20–30 minutes, or until tender. Remove from the oven and keep warm.

Meanwhile, place the eggs in a small saucepan, cover with water and bring to the boil. Simmer for 8 minutes, then drain. Bring a large pan of lightly salted water to a rolling boil. Add the beans and pasta, return to the boil and cook according to the packet instructions, or until 'al dente'. Drain the pasta and beans and refresh under cold running water.

Place the pasta and beans in a bowl, add the carrot, sweetcorn and spinach leaves and toss lightly. Shell the eggs, cut into wedges and arrange on top of the pasta. Slice the duck breasts then place them on top of the salad. Beat the dressing ingredients together in a bowl until well blended, then drizzle over the salad. Serve immediately.

Try this: FOR AN ALTERNATIVE: 122   FOR A LIGHT BITE: 28

Creamy Chicken & Sausage Penne

SERVES 4

2 tbsp olive oil
225 g/8 oz shallots, peeled
8 chicken thighs
175 g/6 oz smoked sausage,
    thickly sliced
125 g/4 oz chestnut
    mushrooms, wiped

and halved
2 garlic cloves, peeled
    and chopped
1 tbsp paprika
1 small bunch fresh thyme,
    chopped, plus leaves
    to garnish

150 ml/¼ pint red wine
300 ml/½ pint chicken stock
freshly ground black pepper
350 g/12 oz penne
250 g carton mascarpone
    cheese

Heat the olive oil in a large frying pan, add the shallots and cook for 3 minutes, or until golden. Remove and drain on absorbent kitchen paper. Add the chicken thighs to the pan and cook for 5 minutes, turning frequently until browned. Drain on absorbent kitchen paper.

Add the smoked sausage and chestnut mushrooms to the pan and cook for 3 minutes, or until browned. Drain separately on absorbent kitchen paper.

Return the shallots, chicken and sausage to the pan, then add the garlic, paprika and thyme and cook for 1 minute, stirring. Pour in the wine and stock and season to taste with black pepper. Bring to the boil, lower the heat and simmer, covered, for 15 minutes. Add the mushrooms to the pan and simmer, covered, for 15 minutes, or until the chicken is tender.

Meanwhile, bring a large pan of lightly salted water to a rolling boil. Add the penne and cook according to the packet instructions, or until 'al dente'. Drain thoroughly.

Stir the mascarpone cheese into the chicken sauce and heat through, stirring gently. Spoon the pasta on to a warmed serving dish, top with the sauce, garnish and serve immediately.

Try this: FOR AN ALTERNATIVE: 196 FOR A LIGHT BITE: 24

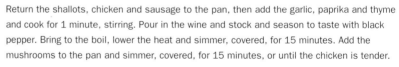

Creamy Turkey & Tomato Pasta

SERVES 4

4 tbsp olive oil
450 g/1 lb turkey breasts, cut
   into bite-sized pieces
550 g/1¼ lb cherry tomatoes,
   on the vine

2 garlic cloves, peeled
   and chopped
4 tbsp balsamic vinegar
4 tbsp freshly chopped basil
salt and freshly ground

   black pepper
200 ml tub crème fraîche
350 g/12 oz tagliatelle
shaved Parmesan cheese,
   to garnish

Preheat the oven to 200°C/400°F/Gas Mark 6. Heat 2 tablespoons of the olive oil in a large frying pan. Add the turkey and cook for 5 minutes, or until sealed, turning occasionally. Transfer to a roasting tin and add the remaining olive oil, the vine tomatoes, garlic and balsamic vinegar. Stir well and season to taste with salt and pepper. Cook in the preheated oven for 30 minutes, or until the turkey is tender, turning the tomatoes and turkey once.

Meanwhile, bring a large pan of lightly salted water to a rolling boil. Add the pasta and cook according to the packet instructions, or until 'al dente'. Drain, return to the pan and keep warm. Stir the basil and seasoning into the crème fraîche.

Remove the roasting tin from the oven and discard the vines. Stir the crème fraîche and basil mix into the turkey and tomato mixture and return to the oven for 1–2 minutes, or until thoroughly heated through.

Stir the turkey and tomato mixture into the pasta and toss lightly together. Tip into a warmed serving dish. Garnish with Parmesan cheese shavings and serve immediately.

Try this: FOR AN ALTERNATIVE: 174 FOR A LIGHT BITE: 34

Parma Ham–wrapped Chicken with Ribbon Pasta

SERVES 4

4 boneless and skinless
   chicken breasts
salt and freshly ground
   black pepper
12 slices Parma ham
2 tbsp olive oil
350 g/12 oz ribbon pasta

1 garlic clove, peeled
   and chopped
1 bunch spring onions,
   trimmed and
   diagonally sliced
400 g can chopped tomatoes
juice of 1 lemon

150 ml/¼ pint crème fraîche
3 tbsp freshly chopped
   parsley
pinch of sugar
freshly grated Parmesan
   cheese, to garnish

Cut each chicken breast into 3 pieces and season well with salt and pepper. Wrap each chicken piece in a slice of Parma ham to enclose completely, securing if necessary with either fine twine or cocktail sticks.

Heat the oil in a large frying pan and cook the chicken, turning occasionally, for 12–15 minutes, or until thoroughly cooked. Remove from the pan with a slotted spoon and reserve.

Meanwhile, bring a large pan of lightly salted water to a rolling boil. Add the pasta and cook according to the packet instructions, or until 'al dente'.

Add the garlic and spring onions to the frying pan and cook, stirring occasionally, for 2 minutes, or until softened. Stir in the tomatoes, lemon juice and crème fraîche. Bring to the boil, lower the heat and simmer, covered, for 3 minutes. Stir in the parsley and sugar, season to taste, then return the chicken to the pan and heat for 2–3 minutes, or until piping hot.

Drain the pasta thoroughly and mix in the chopped parsley, then spoon on to a warmed serving dish or individual plates. Arrange the chicken and sauce over the pasta. Garnish and serve immediately.

Try this: FOR AN ALTERNATIVE: 186   FOR A LIGHT BITE: 58

Baked Aubergines with Tomato & Mozzarella

SERVES 4

3 medium aubergines,
 trimmed and sliced
salt and freshly ground
 black pepper
4–6 tbsp olive oil
450 g/1 lb fresh turkey mince

1 onion, peeled and chopped
2 garlic cloves, peeled
 and chopped
2 x 400 g cans cherry tomatoes
1 tbsp fresh mixed herbs
200 ml/7 fl oz red wine

350 g/12 oz macaroni
5 tbsp freshly chopped basil
125 g/4 oz mozzarella cheese,
 drained and chopped
50 g/2 oz freshly grated
 Parmesan cheese

Preheat the oven to 200°C/400°F/Gas Mark 6, 15 minutes before cooking. Place the aubergine slices in a colander and sprinkle with salt. Leave for 1 hour or until the juices run clear. Rinse and dry on absorbent kitchen paper. Heat 3–5 tablespoons of the olive oil in a large frying pan and cook the prepared aubergines in batches for 2 minutes on each side, or until softened. Remove and drain on absorbent kitchen paper.

Heat 1 tablespoon of olive oil in a saucepan, add the turkey mince and cook for 5 minutes, or until browned and sealed. Add the onion to the pan and cook for 5 minutes, or until softened. Add the chopped garlic, the tomatoes and mixed herbs. Pour in the wine and season to taste with salt and pepper. Bring to the boil, lower the heat then simmer for 15 minutes, or until thickened.

Meanwhile, bring a large pan of lightly salted water to a rolling boil. Add the macaroni and cook according to the packet instructions, or until 'al dente'. Drain thoroughly.

Spoon half the tomato mixture into a lightly oiled ovenproof dish. Top with half the aubergine, pasta and chopped basil, then season lightly. Repeat the layers, finishing with a layer of aubergine. Sprinkle with the mozzarella and Parmesan cheeses, then bake in the preheated oven for 30 minutes, or until golden and bubbling. Serve immediately.

Try this: FOR AN ALTERNATIVE: 240 FOR A LIGHT BITE: 36

Mini Chicken Balls with Tagliatelle

SERVES 4

450 g/1 lb fresh chicken
   mince
50 g/2 oz sun-dried
   tomatoes, drained and
   finely chopped
salt and freshly ground
   black pepper

25 g/1 oz butter
1 tbsp oil
350 g/12 oz leeks, trimmed
   and diagonally sliced
125 g/4 oz frozen broad
   beans
300 ml/½ pint single cream

50 g/2 oz freshly grated
   Parmesan cheese
350 g/12 oz tagliatelle
4 medium eggs
fresh herbs, to garnish

Mix the chicken and tomatoes together and season to taste with salt and pepper. Divide the mixture into 32 pieces and roll into balls. Transfer to a baking sheet, cover and leave in the refrigerator for 1 hour. Melt the butter in a large frying pan, add the chicken balls and cook for 5 minutes, or until golden, turning occasionally. Remove, drain on absorbent kitchen paper and keep warm.

Add the leeks and broad beans to the frying pan and cook, stirring, for 10 minutes or until cooked and tender. Return the chicken balls to the pan, then stir in the cream and Parmesan cheese and heat through.

Meanwhile, bring a large pan of lightly salted water to a rolling boil. Add the pasta and cook according to the packet instructions, or until 'al dente'.

Bring a separate frying pan full of water to the boil, crack in the eggs and simmer for 2–4 minutes, or until poached to personal preference.

Meanwhile, drain the pasta thoroughly and return to the pan. Pour the chicken ball and vegetable sauce over the pasta, toss lightly and heat through for 1–2 minutes. Arrange on warmed individual plates and top with the poached eggs. Garnish with fresh herbs and serve immediately.

Chicken Marengo

SERVES 4

2 tbsp plain flour
salt and freshly ground
  black pepper
4 boneless and skinless
  chicken breasts, cut into
  bite-sized pieces
4 tbsp olive oil

1 Spanish onion, peeled
  and chopped
1 garlic clove, peeled
  and chopped
400 g can chopped tomatoes
2 tbsp sun-dried tomato
  paste

3 tbsp freshly chopped basil
3 tbsp freshly chopped thyme
125 ml/4 fl oz dry white wine
or chicken stock
350 g/12 oz rigatoni
3 tbsp freshly chopped
  flat-leaf parsley

Season the flour with salt and pepper and toss the chicken in the flour to coat. Heat 2 tablespoons of the olive oil in a large frying pan and cook the chicken for 7 minutes, or until browned all over, turning occasionally. Remove from the pan using a slotted spoon and keep warm.

Add the remaining oil to the pan, add the onion and cook, stirring occasionally, for 5 minutes, or until softened and starting to brown. Add the garlic, tomatoes, tomato paste, basil and thyme. Pour in the wine or chicken stock and season well. Bring to the boil. Stir in the chicken pieces and simmer for 15 minutes, or until the chicken is tender and the sauce has thickened.

Meanwhile, bring a large pan of lightly salted water to a rolling boil. Add the rigatoni and cook according to the packet instructions, or until 'al dente'.

Drain the rigatoni thoroughly, return to the pan and stir in the chopped parsley. Tip the pasta into a warmed large serving dish or spoon on to individual plates. Spoon over the chicken sauce and serve immediately.

Try this: FOR AN ALTERNATIVE: 200   FOR A LIGHT BITE: 54

Turkey & Oven-roasted Vegetable Salad

SERVES 4

6 tbsp olive oil

3 medium courgettes, trimmed and sliced

2 yellow peppers, deseeded and sliced

125 g/4 oz pine nuts

275 g/10 oz macaroni

350 g/12 oz cooked turkey

280 g jar or can chargrilled artichokes, drained and sliced

225 g/8 oz baby plum tomatoes, quartered

4 tbsp freshly

chopped coriander

1 garlic clove, peeled and chopped

3 tbsp balsamic vinegar

salt and freshly ground black pepper

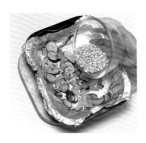

Preheat the oven to 200°C/400°F/Gas Mark 6, 15 minutes before cooking. Line a large roasting tin with tinfoil, pour in half the olive oil and place in the oven for 3 minutes, or until very hot. Remove from the oven, add the courgettes and peppers and stir until evenly coated. Bake for 30–35 minutes, or until slightly charred, turning occasionally.

Add the pine nuts to the tin. Return to the oven and bake for 10 minutes, or until the pine nuts are toasted. Remove from the oven and allow the vegetables to cool completely.

Bring a large pan of lightly salted water to a rolling boil. Add the macaroni and cook according to the packet instructions, or until 'al dente'. Drain and refresh under cold running water then drain thoroughly and place in a large salad bowl.

Cut the turkey into bite-sized pieces and add to the macaroni. Add the artichokes and tomatoes with the cooled vegetables and pan juices to the pan. Blend together the coriander, garlic, remaining oil, vinegar and seasoning. Pour over the salad, toss lightly and serve.

Spicy Chicken & Pasta Salad

SERVES 6

450 g/1 lb pasta shells
25 g/1 oz butter
1 onion, peeled and
   chopped
2 tbsp mild curry paste
125 g/4 oz ready-to-eat dried
   apricots, chopped

2 tbsp tomato paste
3 tbsp mango chutney
300 ml/½ pint mayonnaise
425 g can pineapple slices
   in fruit juice
salt and freshly ground
   black pepper

450 g/1 lb skinned and
   boned cooked chicken, cut
   into bite-sized pieces
25 g/1 oz flaked toasted
   almond slivers
coriander sprigs, to garnish

Bring a large pan of lightly salted water to a rolling boil. Add the pasta shells and cook according to the packet instructions, or until 'al dente'. Drain and refresh under cold running water then drain thoroughly and place in a large serving bowl.

Meanwhile, melt the butter in a heavy-based pan, add the onion and cook for 5 minutes, or until softened. Add the curry paste and cook, stirring, for 2 minutes. Stir in the apricots and tomato paste, then cook for 1 minute. Remove from the heat and allow to cool.

Blend the mango chutney and mayonnaise together in a small bowl. Drain the pineapple slices, adding 2 tablespoons of the pineapple juice to the mayonnaise mixture; reserve the pineapple slices. Season the mayonnaise to taste with salt and pepper.

Cut the pineapple slices into chunks and stir into the pasta together with the mayonnaise mixture, curry paste and cooked chicken pieces. Toss lightly together to coat the pasta. Sprinkle with the almond slivers, garnish with coriander sprigs and serve.

Try this: FOR AN ALTERNATIVE: 296   FOR A LIGHT BITE: 20

Chicken Gorgonzola & Mushroom Macaroni

SERVES 4

450 g/1 lb macaroni
75 g/3 oz butter
225 g/8 oz chestnut
  mushrooms, wiped
  and sliced
225 g/8 oz baby button
  mushrooms, wiped
  and halved

350 g/12 oz cooked chicken,
  skinned and chopped
2 tsp cornflour
300 ml/½ pint semi-
  skimmed milk
50 g/2 oz Gorgonzola
  cheese, chopped, plus
  extra to serve

2 tbsp freshly chopped sage
1 tbsp freshly chopped
  chives, plus extra chive
  leaves to garnish
salt and freshly ground
  black pepper

Bring a large pan of lightly salted water to a rolling boil. Add the macaroni and cook according to the packet instructions, or until 'al dente'.

Meanwhile, melt the butter in a large frying pan, add the chestnut and button mushrooms and cook for 5 minutes, or until golden, stirring occasionally. Add the chicken to the pan and cook for 4 minutes, or until heated through thoroughly and slightly golden, stirring occasionally.

Blend the cornflour with a little of the milk in a jug to form a smooth paste, then gradually blend in the remaining milk and pour into the frying pan. Bring to the boil slowly, stirring constantly. Add cheese and cook for 1 minute, stirring frequently until melted.

Stir the sage and chives into the frying pan. Season to taste with salt and pepper then heat through. Drain the macaroni thoroughly and return to the pan. Pour the chicken and mushroom sauce over the macaroni and toss lightly to coat. Tip into a warmed serving dish, and serve immediately with extra Gorgonzola cheese.

Cheesy Baked
Chicken Macaroni

SERVES 4

1 tbsp olive oil
350 g/12 oz boneless
  and skinless chicken
  breasts, diced
75 g/3 oz pancetta, diced
1 onion, peeled and
  chopped
1 garlic clove, peeled

and chopped
350 g packet fresh
  tomato sauce
400 g can chopped tomatoes
2 tbsp freshly chopped basil,
  plus leaves to garnish
salt and freshly ground
  black pepper

350 g/12 oz macaroni
150 g/5oz mozzarella cheese,
  drained and chopped
50 g/2 oz Gruyère cheese,
  grated
50 g/2 oz freshly grated
  Parmesan cheese

Preheat the grill just before cooking. Heat the oil in large frying pan and cook the chicken for 8 minutes, or until browned, stirring occasionally. Drain on absorbent kitchen paper and reserve. Add the pancetta slices to the pan and fry on both sides until crispy. Remove from the pan and reserve.

Add the onion and garlic to the frying pan and cook for 5 minutes, or until softened. Stir in the tomato sauce, chopped tomatoes and basil and season to taste with salt and pepper. Bring to the boil, lower the heat and simmer the sauce for 5 minutes.

Meanwhile, bring a large pan of lightly salted water to a rolling boil. Add the macaroni and cook according to the packet instructions, or until 'al dente'.

Drain the macaroni thoroughly, return to the pan and stir in the sauce, chicken and mozzarella cheese. Spoon into a shallow ovenproof dish.

Sprinkle the pancetta over the macaroni. Sprinkle over the Gruyère and Parmesan cheeses. Place under the preheated grill and cook for 5–10 minutes, or until golden-brown; turn the dish occasionally. Garnish and serve immediately.

Try this: FOR AN ALTERNATIVE: 282 FOR A LIGHT BITE: 50

Chicken & Prawn–stacked Ravioli

SERVES 4

1 tbsp olive oil
1 onion, peeled and
    chopped
1 garlic clove, peeled
    and chopped
450 g/1 lb boned and
    skinned cooked chicken,

cut into large pieces
1 beefsteak tomato,
    deseeded and chopped
150 ml/¼ pint dry white wine
150 ml/¼ pint double cream
250 g/9 oz peeled cooked
    prawns, thawed if frozen

2 tbsp freshly chopped
    tarragon, plus sprigs
    to garnish
salt and freshly ground
    black pepper
8 sheets fresh lasagne

Heat the olive oil in a large frying pan, add the onion and garlic and cook for 5 minutes, or until softened, stirring occasionally. Add the chicken pieces and fry for 4 minutes, or until heated through, turning occasionally.

Stir in the chopped tomato, wine and cream and bring to the boil. Lower the heat and simmer for about 5 minutes, or until reduced and thickened. Stir in the prawns and tarragon and season to taste with salt and pepper. Heat the sauce through gently.

Meanwhile, bring a large pan of lightly salted water to the boil and add 2 lasagne sheets. Return to the boil and cook for 2 minutes, stirring gently to avoid sticking. Remove from the pan using a slotted spoon and keep warm. Repeat with the remaining sheets.

Cut each sheet of lasagne in half. Place two pieces on each of the warmed plates and divide half of the chicken mixture among them. Top each serving with a second sheet of lasagne and divide the remainder of the chicken mixture among them. Top with a final layer of lasagne. Garnish with tarragon sprigs and serve immediately.

Try this: FOR AN ALTERNATIVE: 302   FOR A LIGHT BITE: 42

Penne with Pan-fried Chicken & Capers

SERVES 4

4 boneless and skinless
  chicken breasts
25 g/1 oz plain flour
salt and freshly ground
  black pepper
350 g/12 oz penne
2 tbsp olive oil
25 g/1 oz butter

1 red onion, peeled
  and sliced
1 garlic clove, peeled
  and chopped
4–6 tbsp pesto
250 g carton mascarpone
  cheese
1 tsp wholegrain mustard

1 tbsp lemon juice
2 tbsp freshly chopped basil
3 tbsp capers in brine, rinsed
  and drained
freshly shaved Pecorino
  Romano cheese

Trim the chicken and cut into bite-sized pieces. Season the flour with salt and pepper then toss the chicken in the seasoned flour and reserve.

Bring a large saucepan of lightly salted water to a rolling boil. Add the penne and cook according to the packet instructions, or until 'al dente'.

Meanwhile, heat the oil in a large frying pan. Add the chicken to the pan and cook for 8 minutes, or until golden on all sides, stirring frequently. Transfer the chicken to a plate and reserve.

Add the onion and garlic to the oil remaining in the frying pan and cook for 5 minutes, or until softened, stirring frequently.

Return the chicken to the frying pan. Stir in the pesto and mascarpone cheese and heat through, stirring gently, until smooth. Stir in the wholegrain mustard, lemon juice, basil and capers. Season to taste, then continue to heat through until piping hot.

Drain the penne thoroughly and return to the saucepan. Pour over the sauce and toss well to coat. Arrange the pasta on warmed plates. Scatter with the cheese and serve immediately.

Try this: FOR AN ALTERNATIVE: 166   FOR A LIGHT BITE: 56

Vegetables & Salads

Melanzane Parmigiana

SERVES 4

900 g/2 lb aubergines
salt and freshly ground
   black pepper
5 tbsp olive oil
1 red onion, peeled
   and chopped
½ tsp mild paprika pepper

150 ml/¼ pint dry red wine
150 ml/¼ pint vegetable stock
400 g can chopped tomatoes
1 tsp tomato purée
1 tbsp freshly chopped
   oregano
175 g/6 oz mozzarella

cheese, thinly sliced
40 g/1½ oz Parmesan
   cheese, coarsely grated
sprig of fresh basil,
   to garnish

Preheat oven to 200°C/400°F/Gas Mark 6, 15 minutes before cooking. Cut the aubergines lengthways into thin slices. Sprinkle with salt and leave to drain in a colander over a bowl for 30 minutes.

Meanwhile, heat 1 tablespoon of the olive oil in a saucepan and fry the onion for 10 minutes, until softened. Add the paprika and cook for 1 minute. Stir in the wine, stock, tomatoes and tomato purée. Simmer, uncovered, for 25 minutes, or until fairly thick. Stir in the oregano and season to taste with salt and pepper. Remove from the heat.

Rinse the aubergine slices thoroughly under cold water and pat dry on absorbent kitchen paper. Heat 2 tablespoons of the oil in a griddle pan and cook the aubergines in batches, for 3 minutes on each side, until golden. Drain well on absorbent kitchen paper.

Pour half of the tomato sauce into the base of a large ovenproof dish. Cover with half the aubergine slices, then top with the mozzarella. Cover with the remaining aubergine slices and pour over the remaining tomato sauce. Sprinkle with the grated Parmesan cheese.

Bake in the preheated oven for 30 minutes, or until the aubergines are tender and the sauce is bubbling. Garnish with a sprig of fresh basil and cool for a few minutes before serving.

Stuffed Tomatoes with Grilled Polenta

SERVES 4

For the polenta:
300 ml/½ pint vegetable
  stock
salt and freshly ground
  black pepper
50 g/2 oz quick-cook polenta
15 g/½ oz butter

For the stuffed tomatoes:
4 large tomatoes
1 tbsp olive oil
1 garlic clove, peeled
  and crushed
1 bunch spring onions,
  trimmed and
  finely chopped

2 tbsp freshly chopped
  parsley
2 tbsp freshly chopped basil
2 slices Parma ham, cut into
  thin slivers
50 g/2 oz fresh white
  breadcrumbs
snipped chives, to garnish

Preheat grill just before cooking. To make the polenta, pour the stock into a saucepan. Add a pinch of salt and bring to the boil. Pour in the polenta in a fine stream, stirring all the time. Simmer for about 15 minutes, or until very thick. Stir in the butter and add a little pepper. Turn the polenta out on to a chopping board and spread to a thickness of just over 1 cm/½ inch. Cool, cover with clingfilm and chill in the refrigerator for 30 minutes.

To make the stuffed tomatoes, cut the tomatoes in half then scoop out the seeds and press through a fine sieve to extract the juices. Season the insides of the tomatoes with salt and pepper and reserve. Heat the olive oil in a saucepan and gently fry the garlic and spring onions for 3 minutes. Add the tomatoes' juices, bubble for 3–4 minutes, until most of the liquid has evaporated. Stir in the herbs, Parma ham and a little black pepper with half the breadcrumbs. Spoon into the hollowed out tomatoes and reserve.

Cut the polenta into 5 cm/2 inch squares, then cut again to make triangles. Put the triangles on a piece of tinfoil on the grill rack and grill for 4–5 minutes on each side, until golden. Cover and keep warm. Grill the tomatoes under a medium-hot grill for about 4 minutes – any exposed Parma ham will become crisp. Sprinkle with the remaining breadcrumbs and grill for 1–2 minutes, or until the breadcrumbs are golden brown. Garnish with snipped chives and serve immediately with the grilled polenta.

Try this FOR AN ALTERNATIVE: 246 FOR A LIGHT BITE: 56

Rigatoni with Roasted Beetroot & Rocket

SERVES 4

350 g/12 oz raw baby
  beetroot, unpeeled
1 garlic clove, peeled
  and crushed
½ tsp finely grated

orange rind
1 tbsp orange juice
1 tsp lemon juice
2 tbsp walnut oil
salt and freshly ground

black pepper
350 g/12 oz dried fettucini
75 g/3 oz rocket leaves
125 g/4 oz Dolcelatte cheese,
  cut into small cubes

Preheat oven to 150°C/300°F/Gas Mark 2, 10 minutes before cooking. Wrap the beetroot individually in tinfoil and bake for 1–1½ hours, or until tender. (Test by opening one of the parcels and scraping the skin away from the stem end – it should come off very easily.)

Leave the beetroot until cool enough to handle, then peel and cut each beetroot into 6–8 wedges, depending on the size. Mix the garlic, orange rind and juice, lemon juice, walnut oil and salt and pepper together, then drizzle over the beetroot and toss to coat well.

Meanwhile, bring a large saucepan of lightly salted water to the boil. Cook the pasta for 10 minutes, or until 'al dente'.

Drain the pasta thoroughly, then add the warm beetroot, rocket leaves and Dolcelatte cheese. Quickly and gently toss together, then divide between serving bowls and serve immediately before the rocket wilts.

Mixed Salad with Anchovy Dressing & Ciabatta Croûtons

SERVES 4

1 small head endive
1 small head chicory
1 fennel bulb
400 g can artichokes,
   drained and rinsed
½ cucumber
125 g/4 oz cherry tomatoes

75 g/3 oz black olives

For the anchovy dressing:
50 g can anchovy fillets
1 tsp Dijon mustard
1 small garlic clove, peeled
   and crushed

4 tbsp olive oil
1 tbsp lemon juice
freshly ground black pepper

For the ciabatta croûtons:
2 thick slices ciabatta bread
2 tbsp olive oil

Divide the endive and chicory into leaves and reserve some of the larger ones. Arrange the smaller leaves in a wide salad bowl.

Cut the fennel bulb in half from the stalk to the root end, then cut across in fine slices. Quarter the artichokes, then quarter and slice the cucumber and halve the tomatoes. Add to the salad bowl with the olives.

To make the dressing, drain the anchovies and put in a blender with the mustard, garlic, olive oil, lemon juice, 2 tablespoons of hot water and black pepper. Whiz together until smooth and thickened.

To make the croûtons, cut the bread into 1 cm/½ inch cubes. Heat the oil in a frying pan, add the bread cubes and fry for 3 minutes, turning frequently until golden. Remove and drain on absorbent kitchen paper.

Drizzle half the anchovy dressing over the prepared salad and toss to coat. Arrange the reserved endive and chicory leaves around the edge, then drizzle over the remaining dressing. Scatter over the croûtons and serve immediately.

Rice–filled Peppers

SERVES 4

8 ripe tomatoes
2 tbsp olive oil
1 onion, peeled and
    chopped
1 garlic clove, peeled
    and crushed

½ tsp dark muscovado sugar
125 g/4 oz cooked
    long-grain rice
50 g/2 oz pine nuts, toasted
1 tbsp freshly chopped
    oregano

salt and freshly ground
    black pepper
2 large red peppers
2 large yellow peppers
mixed salad, to serve
crusty bread, to serve

Preheat oven to 200°C/400°F/Gas Mark 6. Put the tomatoes in a small bowl and pour over boiling water to cover. Leave for 1 minute, then drain. Plunge the tomatoes into cold water to cool, then peel off the skins. Quarter, remove the seeds and chop.

Heat the olive oil in a frying pan, and cook the onion gently for 10 minutes, until softened. Add the garlic, chopped tomatoes and sugar.

Gently cook the tomato mixture for 10 minutes until thickened. Remove from the heat and stir the rice, pine nuts and oregano into the sauce. Season to taste with salt and pepper.

Halve the peppers lengthways, cutting through and leaving the stem on. Remove the seeds and cores, then put the peppers in a lightly oiled roasting tin, cut-side down and cook in the preheated oven for about 10 minutes.

Turn the peppers so they are cut side up. Spoon in the filling, then cover with tinfoil. Return to the oven for 15 minutes, or until the peppers are very tender, removing the tinfoil for the last 5 minutes to allow the tops to brown a little.

Serve 1 red pepper half and 1 yellow pepper half per person with a mixed salad and plenty of warmed, crusty bread.

Try this: FOR AN ALTERNATIVE: 240 FOR A LIGHT BITE: 20

Rigatoni with Oven–dried Cherry Tomatoes & Mascarpone

SERVES 4

350 g/12 oz red cherry
   tomatoes
1 tsp caster sugar
salt and freshly ground
   black pepper

2 tbsp olive oil
400 g/14 oz dried rigatoni
125 g/4 oz petits pois
2 tbsp mascarpone cheese
1 tbsp freshly chopped mint

1 tbsp freshly chopped
   parsley
sprigs of fresh mint,
   to garnish

Preheat oven to 140°C/275°F/Gas Mark 1. Halve the cherry tomatoes and place close together on a non-stick baking tray, cut-side up. Sprinkle lightly with the sugar, then with a little salt and pepper. Bake in the preheated oven for 1¼ hours, or until dry, but not beginning to colour. Leave to cool on the baking tray. Put in a bowl, drizzle over the olive oil and toss to coat.

Bring a large saucepan of lightly salted water to the boil and cook the pasta for about 10 minutes or until 'al dente'. Add the petits pois, 2–3 minutes before the end of the cooking time. Drain thoroughly and return the pasta and the petits pois to the saucepan.

Add the mascarpone to the saucepan. When melted, add the tomatoes, mint, parsley and a little black pepper. Toss gently together, then transfer to a warmed serving dish or individual plates and garnish with sprigs of fresh mint. Serve immediately.

Try this: FOR AN ALTERNATIVE: 288   FOR A LIGHT BITE: 20

Red Pepper & Basil Tart

SERVES 4–6

For the olive pastry:
225 g/8 oz plain flour
pinch of salt
50 g/2 oz pitted black olives,
  finely chopped
1 medium egg, lightly
  beaten, plus 1 egg yolk

3 tbsp olive oil

For the filling:
2 large red peppers,
  quartered and deseeded
175 g/6 oz mascarpone
  cheese

4 tbsp milk
2 medium eggs
3 tbsp freshly chopped basil
salt and freshly ground black
  pepper
sprig of fresh basil, to garnish
mixed salad, to serve

Preheat oven to 200°C/400°F/Gas Mark 6, 15 minutes before cooking. Sift the flour and salt into a bowl. Make a well in the centre. Stir together the egg, oil and 1 tablespoon of tepid water. Add to the dry ingredients, drop in the olives and mix to a dough. Knead on a lightly floured surface for a few seconds until smooth, then wrap in clingfilm and chill in the refrigerator for 30 minutes.

Roll out the pastry and use to line a 23 cm/9 inch loose-bottomed fluted flan tin. Lightly prick the base with a fork. Cover and chill in the refrigerator for 20 minutes.

Cook the peppers under a hot grill for 10 minutes, or until the skins are blackened and blistered. Put the peppers in a plastic bag, cool for 10 minutes, then remove the skin and slice.

Line the pastry case with tinfoil or greaseproof paper weighed down with baking beans and bake in the preheated oven for 10 minutes. Remove the tinfoil and beans and bake for a further 5 minutes. Reduce the oven temperature to 180°C/350°F/Gas Mark 4.

Beat the mascarpone cheese until smooth. Gradually add the milk and eggs. Stir in the peppers, basil and season to taste with salt and pepper. Spoon into the flan case and bake for 25–30 minutes, or until lightly set. Garnish with a sprig of fresh basil and serve immediately with a mixed salad.

Try this: FOR AN ALTERNATIVE: 208 FOR A LIGHT BITE: 20

Spinach Dumplings with Rich Tomato Sauce

SERVES 4

For the sauce:
2 tbsp olive oil
1 onion, peeled and
   chopped
1 garlic clove, peeled
   and crushed
1 red chilli, deseeded
   and chopped
150 ml/¼ pint dry white wine
400 g can chopped tomatoes

pared strip of lemon rind

For the dumplings:
450 g/1 lb fresh spinach
50 g/2 oz ricotta cheese
25 g/1 oz fresh white
   breadcrumbs
25 g/1 oz Parmesan
   cheese, grated
1 medium egg yolk

¼ tsp freshly grated nutmeg
salt and freshly ground
   black pepper
5 tbsp plain flour
2 tbsp olive oil, for frying
fresh basil leaves, to garnish
freshly cooked tagliatelle,
   to serve

To make the tomato sauce, heat the olive oil in a large saucepan and fry the onion gently for 5 minutes. Add the garlic and chilli and cook for a further 5 minutes, until softened.

Stir in the wine, chopped tomatoes and lemon rind. Bring to the boil, cover and simmer for 20 minutes, then uncover and simmer for 15 minutes, or until the sauce has thickened. Remove the lemon rind and season to taste with salt and pepper.

To make the spinach dumplings, wash the spinach thoroughly and remove any tough stalks. Cover and cook in a large saucepan over a low heat with just the water clinging to the leaves. Drain, then squeeze out all the excess water. Finely chop and put in a large bowl.

Add the ricotta, breadcrumbs, Parmesan cheeseand egg yolk to the spinach. Season with nutmeg and salt and pepper. Mix together and shape into 20 walnut-sized balls.

Toss the spinach balls in the flour. Heat the olive oil in a large non-stick frying pan and fry the balls gently for 5–6 minutes, carefully turning occasionally. Garnish with fresh basil leaves and serve immediately with the tomato sauce and tagliatelle.

Try this: FOR AN ALTERNATIVE: 300 FOR A LIGHT BITE: 60

Venetian–style Vegetables & Beans

SERVES 4

250 g/9 oz dried pinto beans
3 sprigs of fresh parsley
1 sprig of fresh rosemary
2 tbsp olive oil
200 g can chopped tomatoes
2 shallots, peeled

For the vegetable mixture:
1 large red onion, peeled
1 large white onion, peeled
1 medium carrot, peeled
2 sticks celery, trimmed
3 tbsp olive oil

3 bay leaves
1 tsp caster sugar
3 tbsp red wine vinegar
salt and freshly ground
    black pepper

Put the beans in a bowl, cover with plenty of cold water and leave to soak for at least 8 hours, or overnight.

Drain and rinse the beans. Put in a large saucepan with 1.1 litres/2 pints cold water. Tie the parsley and rosemary in muslin and add to the beans with the olive oil. Boil rapidly for 10 minutes, then lower the heat and simmer for 20 minutes with the saucepan half-covered. Stir in the tomatoes and shallots and simmer for a further 10–15 minutes, or until the beans are cooked.

Meanwhile, slice the red and white onion into rings and then finely dice the carrot and celery. Heat the olive oil in a saucepan and cook the onions over a very low heat for about 10 minutes. Add the carrot, celery and bay leaves to the saucepan and cook for a further 10 minutes, stirring frequently, until the vegetables are tender. Sprinkle with sugar, stir and cook for 1 minute.

Stir in the vinegar. Cook for 1 minute, then remove the saucepan from the heat. Drain the beans through a fine sieve, discarding all the herbs, then add the beans to the onion mixture and season well with salt and pepper. Mix gently, then tip the beans into a large serving bowl. Leave to cool, then serve at room temperature.

Try this: FOR AN ALTERNATIVE: 266 FOR A LIGHT BITE: 18

Roast Butternut Squash Risotto

SERVES 4

1 medium butternut squash
2 tbsp olive oil
1 garlic bulb, cloves
   separated, but unpeeled
15 g/½ oz unsalted butter
275 g/10 oz Arborio rice
large pinch of saffron
   strands

150 ml/¼ pint dry white wine
1 litre/1¾ pints
   vegetable stock
1 tbsp freshly
   chopped parsley
1 tbsp freshly
   chopped oregano
50 g/2 oz Parmesan cheese,

finely grated
salt and freshly ground
   black pepper
sprigs of fresh oregano,
   to garnish
extra Parmesan cheese,
   to serve

Preheat oven to 190°C/375°F/Gas Mark 5. Cut the butternut squash in half, thickly peel, then scoop out the seeds and discard. Cut the flesh into 2 cm/¾ inch cubes.

Pour the oil into a large roasting tin and heat in the oven for 5 minutes. Add the butternut squash and garlic cloves. Turn in the oil to coat, then roast in the oven for about 25–30 minutes, or until golden brown and very tender, turning the vegetables halfway through cooking time.

Melt the butter in a large saucepan. Add the rice and stir over a high heat for a few seconds. Add the saffron and the wine and bubble fiercely until almost totally reduced, stirring frequently. At the same time heat the stock in a separate saucepan and keep at a steady simmer. Reduce the heat under the rice to low. Add a ladleful of stock to the saucepan and simmer, stirring, until absorbed. Continue adding the stock in this way until the rice is tender. This will take about 20 minutes and it may not be necessary to add all the stock.

Turn off the heat, stir in the herbs, Parmesan cheese and seasoning. Cover and leave to stand for 2–3 minutes. Quickly remove the skins from the roasted garlic. Add to the risotto with the butternut squash and mix gently. Garnish with sprigs of oregano and serve immediately with Parmesan cheese.

Try this: FOR AN ALTERNATIVE: 128 FOR A LIGHT BITE: 24

Aubergine Cannelloni with Watercress Sauce

SERVES 4

4 large aubergines, about
    250 g/9 oz each
5–6 tbsp olive oil
350 g/12 oz ricotta cheese
75 g/3 oz Parmesan
    cheese, grated
3 tbsp freshly chopped basil

salt and freshly ground
    black pepper

For the watercress sauce:
75 g/3 oz watercress, trimmed
200 ml/⅓ pint vegetable stock
1 shallot, peeled and sliced

pared strip of lemon rind
1 large sprig of thyme
3 tbsp crème fraîche
1 tsp lemon juice

sprigs of watercress, to garnish
lemon zest, to garnish

Preheat oven to 190°C/375°F/Gas Mark 5, 10 minutes before cooking. Cut the aubergines lengthways into thin slices, discarding the side pieces. Heat 2 tablespoons of oil in a frying pan and cook the aubergine slices in a single layer in several batches, turning once, until golden on both sides.

Mix the cheeses, basil and seasoning together. Lay the aubergine slices on a clean surface and spread the cheese mixture evenly between them. Roll up the slices from one of the short ends to enclose the filling. Place, seam-side down in a single layer in an ovenproof dish. Bake in the preheated oven for 15 minutes, or until golden.

To make the watercress sauce, blanch the watercress leaves in boiling water for about 30 seconds. Drain well, then rinse in a sieve under cold running water and squeeze dry. Put the stock, shallot, lemon rind and thyme in a small saucepan. Boil rapidly until reduced by half, then remove from the heat and strain. Put the watercress and strained stock in a food processor and blend until fairly smooth. Return to the saucepan, stir in the crème fraîche, lemon juice and season to taste with salt and pepper. Heat gently until the sauce is piping hot.

Serve a little of the sauce drizzled over the aubergines and the rest separately in a jug. Garnish the cannelloni with sprigs of watercress and lemon zest. Serve immediately.

Try this: FOR AN ALTERNATIVE: 238   FOR A LIGHT BITE: 48

Panzanella

SERVES 4

250 g/9 oz day-old
   Italian-style bread
1 tbsp red wine vinegar
4 tbsp olive oil
1 tsp lemon juice
1 small garlic clove, peeled
   and finely chopped

1 red onion, peeled and
   finely sliced
1 cucumber, peeled
   if preferred
225 g/8 oz ripe tomatoes,
   deseeded
150 g/5 oz pitted black olives

about 20 basil leaves,
   coarsely torn or left
   whole if small
sea salt and freshly ground
   black pepper

Cut the bread into thick slices, leaving the crusts on. Add 1 teaspoon of red wine vinegar to a jug of iced water, put the slices of bread in a bowl and pour over the water. Make sure the bread is covered completely. Leave to soak for 3–4 minutes until just soft.

Remove the soaked bread from the water and squeeze it gently, first with your hands and then in a clean tea towel to remove any excess water. Put the bread on a plate, cover with clingfilm and chill in the refrigerator for about 1 hour.

Meanwhile, whisk together the olive oil, the remaining red wine vinegar and lemon juice in a large serving bowl. Add the garlic and onion and stir to coat well.

Halve the cucumber and remove the seeds. Chop both the cucumber and tomatoes into 1 cm/½ inch dice. Add to the garlic and onions with the olives. Tear the bread into bite-sized chunks and add to the bowl with the fresh basil leaves. Toss together to mix and serve immediately, with a grinding of sea salt and black pepper.

Vegetable Frittata

SERVES 2

6 medium eggs
2 tbsp freshly chopped
 parsley
1 tbsp freshly chopped
 tarragon
25 g/1 oz pecorino or
 Parmesan cheese,

finely grated
freshly ground black pepper
175 g/6 oz tiny new potatoes
2 small carrots, peeled
 and sliced
125 g/4 oz broccoli, cut into
 small florets

1 courgette, about
 125 g/4 oz, sliced
2 tbsp olive oil
4 spring onions, trimmed
 and thinly sliced
mixed green salad, to serve
crusty Italian bread, to serve

Preheat grill just before cooking. Lightly beat the eggs with the parsley, tarragon and half the cheese. Season to taste with black pepper and reserve. (Salt is not needed as the pecorino is very salty.)

Bring a large saucepan of lightly salted water to the boil. Add the new potatoes and cook for 8 minutes. Add the carrots and cook for 4 minutes, then add the broccoli florets and the courgettes and cook for a further 3–4 minutes, or until all the vegetables are barely tender. Drain well.

Heat the oil in a 20.5 cm/8 inch heavy-based frying pan. Add the spring onions and cook for 3–4 minutes, or until softened. Add all the vegetables and cook for a few seconds, then pour in the beaten egg mixture. Stir gently for about a minute, then cook for a further 1–2 minutes, or until the bottom of the frittata is set and golden brown.

Place the pan under a hot grill for 1 minute, or until almost set and just beginning to brown. Sprinkle with the remaining cheese and grill for a further 1 minute, or until it is lightly browned.

Loosen the edges and slide out of the pan. Cut into wedges and serve hot or warm with a mixed green salad and crusty Italian bread.

Try this: FOR AN ALTERNATIVE: 108 FOR A LIGHT BITE: 30

Panzerotti

SERVES 16

450 g/1 lb strong white flour
pinch of salt
1 tsp easy-blend dried yeast
2 tbsp olive oil
300 ml/½ pint warm water
fresh rocket leaves, to serve

For the filling:
1 tbsp olive oil

1 small red onion, peeled
  and finely chopped
2 garlic cloves, peeled
  and crushed
½ yellow pepper, deseeded
  and chopped
1 small courgette, about
  75 g/3 oz, trimmed
  and chopped

50 g/2 oz black olives, pitted
  and quartered
125 g/4 oz mozzarella
  cheese, cut into tiny cubes
salt and freshly ground
  black pepper
5–6 tbsp tomato purée
1 tsp dried mixed herbs
oil for deep-frying

Sift the flour and salt into a bowl. Stir in the yeast. Make a well in the centre. Add the oil and the warm water and mix to a soft dough. Knead on a lightly floured surface until smooth and elastic. Put in an oiled bowl, cover and leave in a warm place to rise while making the filling.

To make the filling, heat the oil in a frying pan and cook the onion for 5 minutes. Add the garlic, yellow pepper and courgette. Cook for about 5 minutes, or until the vegetables are tender. Tip into a bowl and leave to cool slightly. Stir in the olives, mozzarella cheese and season to taste with salt and pepper.

Briefly reknead the dough. Divide into 16 equal pieces. Roll out each to a circle about 10 cm/ 4 inches. Mix together the tomato purée and dried herbs, then spread about 1 teaspoon on each circle, leaving a 2 cm/¾ inch border around the edge. Divide the filling equally between the circles, it will seem a small amount, but if you overfill, they will leak during cooking. Brush the edges with water, then fold in half to enclose the filling. Press to seal, then crimp the edges.

Heat the oil in a deep-fat fryer to 180°C/350°F. Deep-fry the panzerotti in batches for 3 minutes, or until golden. Drain on absorbent kitchen paper and keep warm in a low oven until ready to serve with fresh rocket.

Try this: FOR AN ALTERNATIVE: 260 FOR A LIGHT BITE: 28

Pasta Primavera

SERVES 4

150 g/5 oz French beans
150 g/5 oz sugar snap peas
40 g/1½ oz butter
1 tsp olive oil
225 g/8 oz baby carrots,
   scrubbed
2 courgettes, trimmed
   and thinly sliced

175 g/6 oz baby leeks,
   trimmed and cut into
   2.5 cm/1 inch lengths
200 ml/7 fl oz double cream
1 tsp finely grated
   lemon rind
350 g/12 oz dried tagliatelle
25 g/1 oz Parmesan

cheese, grated
1 tbsp freshly snipped
   chives
1 tbsp freshly chopped dill
salt and freshly ground
   black pepper
sprigs of fresh dill,
   to garnish

Trim and halve the French beans. Bring a large saucepan of lightly salted water to the boil and cook the beans for 4–5 minutes, adding the sugar snap peas after 2 minutes, so that both are tender at the same time. Drain the beans and sugar snap peas and briefly rinse under cold running water. Heat the butter and oil in a large non-stick frying pan. Add the baby carrots and cook for 2 minutes, then stir in the courgettes and leeks and cook for 10 minutes, stirring, until the vegetables are almost tender.

Stir the cream and lemon rind into the vegetables and bubble over a gentle heat until the sauce is slightly reduced and the vegetables are cooked. Meanwhile, bring a large saucepan of lightly salted water to the boil and cook the tagliatelle for 10 minutes, or until 'al dente'.

Add the beans, sugar snaps, Parmesan cheese and herbs to the sauce. Stir for 30 seconds, or until the cheese has melted and the vegetables are hot.

Drain the tagliatelle, add the vegetables and sauce, then toss gently to mix and season to taste with salt and pepper. Spoon into a warmed serving bowl and garnish with a few sprigs of dill and serve immediately.

Try this: FOR AN ALTERNATIVE: 254 FOR A LIGHT BITE: 26

Spaghetti with Pesto

SERVES 4

200 g/7 oz freshly grated
  Parmesan cheese, plus
  extra to serve
25 g/1 oz fresh basil leaves,
  plus extra to garnish

6 tbsp pine nuts
3 large garlic cloves, peeled
200 ml/7 fl oz extra virgin
  olive oil, plus more
  if necessary

salt and freshly ground
  pepper
400 g/14 oz spaghetti

To make the pesto, place the Parmesan cheese in a food processor with the basil leaves, pine nuts and garlic and process until well blended.

With the motor running, gradually pour in the extra virgin olive oil, until a thick sauce forms. Add a little more oil if the sauce seems too thick. Season to taste with salt and pepper. Transfer to a bowl, cover and store in the refrigerator until required.

Bring a large pan of lightly salted water to a rolling boil. Add the spaghetti and cook according to the packet instructions, or until 'al dente'.

Drain the spaghetti thoroughly and return to the pan. Stir in the pesto and toss lightly. Heat through gently, then tip the pasta into a warmed serving dish or spoon on to individual plates. Garnish with basil leaves and serve immediately with extra Parmesan cheese.

Try this: FOR AN ALTERNATIVE: 274 FOR A LIGHT BITE: 38

Pasta Shells with Broccoli & Capers

SERVES 4

400 g/14 oz conchiglie
(shells)
450 g/1 lb broccoli florets,
cut into small pieces
5 tbsp olive oil
1 large onion, peeled and
finely chopped

4 tbsp capers in brine, rinsed
and drained
½ tsp dried chilli flakes
(optional)
75 g/3 oz freshly grated
Parmesan cheese, plus
extra to serve

25 g/1 oz pecorino
cheese, grated
salt and freshly ground
black pepper
2 tbsp freshly chopped
flat-leaf parsley,
to garnish

Bring a large pan of lightly salted water to a rolling boil. Add the orecchiette, return to the boil and cook for 2 minutes. Add the broccoli to the pan. Return to the boil and continue cooking for 8–10 minutes, or until the conchiglie is 'al dente'.

Meanwhile, heat the olive oil in a large frying pan, add the onion and cook for 5 minutes, or until softened, stirring frequently. Stir in the capers and chilli flakes, if using, and cook for a further 2 minutes.

Drain the pasta and broccoli and add to the frying pan. Toss the ingredients to mix thoroughly. Sprinkle over the cheeses, then stir until the cheeses have just melted. Season to taste with salt and pepper, then tip into a warmed serving dish. Garnish with chopped parsley and serve immediately with extra Parmesan cheese.

Cheesy Pasta with Tomatoes & Cream

SERVES 4

225 g/8 oz fresh ricotta cheese	2–3 tbsp finely chopped mint, basil or parsley	2 garlic cloves, peeled and finely chopped
225 g/8 oz smoked mozzarella, grated, (use normal if smoked is unavailable)	salt and freshly ground black pepper	450g/1 lb ripe plum tomatoes, peeled, deseeded and finely chopped
5 g/4 oz freshly grated pecorino or Parmesan cheese	**For the sauce:** 2 tbsp olive oil	50 ml/2 fl oz white vermouth 225 ml/8 fl oz double cream
2 medium eggs, lightly beaten	1 small onion, peeled and finely chopped	fresh basil leaves, to garnish

Place the ricotta cheese in a bowl and beat until smooth, then add the remaining cheeses with the eggs, herbs and seasoning to taste. Beat well until creamy and smooth.

Cut the prepared pasta dough into quarters. Working with one-quarter at a time, and covering the remaining quarters with a clean, damp tea towel, roll out the pasta very thinly. Using a 10 cm/4 inch pastry cutter or small saucer, cut out as many rounds as possible.

Place a small tablespoonful of the filling mixture slightly below the centre of each round. Lightly moisten the edge of the round with water and fold in half to form a filled half-moon shape. Using a dinner fork, press the edges together firmly. Transfer to a lightly floured baking sheet and continue filling the remaining pasta. Leave to dry for 15 minutes.

Heat the oil in a large saucepan, add the onions and cook for 3–4 minutes, or until beginning to soften. Add the garlic and cook for 1–2 minutes, then add the tomatoes, vermouth and cream and bring to the boil. Simmer for 10–15 minutes, or until thickened and reduced. Bring a large saucepan of salted water to the boil. Add the filled pasta and return to the boil. Cook, stirring frequently to prevent sticking, for 5 minutes, or until 'al dente'. Drain and return to the pan. Pour over the tomato and cream sauce, garnish with basil leaves and serve immediately

Try this: FOR AN ALTERNATIVE: 288 FOR A LIGHT BITE: 30

Linguine with Walnut Pesto

SERVES 4

125 g/4 oz walnut halves
1-2 garlic cloves, peeled and
    coarsely chopped
40 g/1½ oz dried
    breadcrumbs
3 tbsp extra virgin olive oil

1 tbsp walnut oil
3-4 tbsp freshly chopped
    parsley
50 g/2 oz butter, softened
2 tbsp double cream
25 g/1 oz Parmesan cheese,

grated, plus extra to serve
salt and freshly ground
    black pepper
450 g/1 lb linguine

Bring a saucepan of water to the boil. Add the walnut halves and simmer for about 1 minute. Drain and turn on to a clean tea towel. Using the towel, rub the nuts gently to loosen the skins, turn into a coarse sieve or colander and shake to separate the skins. Discard the skins and coarsely chop the nuts.

With the the food processor motor running, drop in the garlic cloves and chop finely. Remove the lid, then add the walnuts, breadcrumbs, olive and walnut oils and the parsley. Blend to a paste with a crumbly texture.

Scrape the nut mixture into a bowl, add the softened butter and, using a wooden spoon, cream them together. Gradually beat in the cream and the Parmesan cheese. Season the walnut pesto to taste with salt and pepper.

Bring a large pan of lightly salted water to a rolling boil. Add the linguine and cook according to the packet instructions, or until 'al dente'.

Drain the linguine thoroughly, reserving 1–2 tablespoons of the cooking water. Return the linguine and reserved water to the pan. Add the walnut pesto, 1 tablespoon at a time, tossing and stirring until well coated. Tip into a warmed serving dish or spoon on to individual plates. Serve immediately with the extra grated Parmesan cheese.

Try this: FOR AN ALTERNATIVE: 308   FOR A LIGHT BITE: 58

Four-cheese Tagliatelle

SERVES 4

300 ml/½ pint whipping cream
4 garlic cloves, peeled and
   lightly bruised
75 g/3 oz fontina
   cheese, diced
75 g/3 oz Gruyère

cheese, grated
75 g/3 oz mozzarella cheese,
   preferably, diced
50 g/2 oz Parmesan cheese,
   grated, plus extra to serve
salt and freshly ground

black pepper
275 g/10 oz fresh green
   tagliatelle
1–2 tbsp freshly snipped
   chives
fresh basil leaves, to garnish

Place the whipping cream with the garlic cloves in a medium pan and heat gently until small bubbles begin to form around the edge of the pan. Using a slotted spoon, remove and discard the garlic cloves.

Add all the cheeses to the pan and stir until melted. Season with a little salt and a lot of black pepper. Keep the sauce warm over a low heat, but do not allow to boil.

Meanwhile, bring a large pan of lightly salted water to the boil. Add the taglietelle, return to the boil and cook for 2–3 minutes, or until 'al dente'.

Drain the pasta thoroughly and return to the pan. Pour the sauce over the pasta, add the chives then toss lightly until well coated. Tip into a warmed serving dish or spoon on to individual plates. Garnish with a few basil leaves and serve immediately with extra Parmesan cheese.

Try this: FOR AN ALTERNATIVE: 272   FOR A LIGHT BITE: 52

Spaghetti alla Puttanesca

SERVES 4

4 tbsp olive oil	400 g can chopped	chopped oregano
50 g/2 oz anchovy fillets in	plum tomatoes	1 tbsp tomato paste
olive oil, drained and	125 g/4 oz pitted black	salt and freshly ground
coarsely chopped	olives, cut in half	black pepper
2 garlic cloves, peeled and	2 tbsp capers, rinsed	400 g/14 oz spaghetti
finely chopped	and drained	2 tbsp freshly
½ tsp crushed dried chillies	1 tsp freshly	chopped parsley

Heat the olive oil in a large frying pan, add the anchovies and cook, stirring with a wooden spoon and crushing the anchovies, until they disintegrate. Add the garlic and dried chillies and cook for 1 minute, stirring frequently.

Add the tomatoes, olives, capers, oregano and tomato paste and cook, stirring occasionally, for 15 minutes, or until the liquid has evaporated and the sauce is thickened. Season the tomato sauce to taste with salt and pepper.

Meanwhile, bring a large pan of lightly salted water to a rolling boil. Add the spaghetti and cook according to the packet instructions, or until 'al dente'.

Drain the spaghetti thoroughly, reserving 1–2 tablespoons of the the cooking water. Return the spaghetti with the reserved water to the pan. Pour the tomato sauce over the spaghetti, add the chopped parsley and toss to coat. Tip into a warmed serving dish or spoon on to individual plates and serve immediately.

Try this: FOR AN ALTERNATIVE: 104 FOR A LIGHT BITE: 56

Courgette Lasagne

SERVES 8

2 tbsp olive oil
1 medium onion, peeled and finely chopped
225 g/8 oz mushrooms, wiped and thinly sliced
3–4 courgettes, trimmed and thinly sliced
2 garlic cloves, peeled and finely chopped
½ tsp dried thyme
1–2 tbsp freshly chopped basil or flat-leaf parsley
salt and freshly ground black pepper
1 quantity prepared white sauce (see page 136)
350 g/12 oz lasagne sheets, cooked
225 g/8 oz mozzarella cheese, grated
50 g/2 oz Parmesan cheese, grated
400 g can chopped tomatoes, drained

Preheat the oven to 200°C/400°F/Gas Mark 6, 15 minutes before cooking. Heat the oil in a large frying pan, add the onion and cook for 3–5 minutes. Add the mushrooms, cook for 2 minutes then add the courgettes and cook for a further 3–4 minutes, or until tender. Stir in the garlic, thyme and basil or parsley and season to taste with salt and pepper. Remove from the heat and reserve.

Spoon one-third of the white sauce on to the base of a lightly oiled large baking dish. Arrange a layer of lasagne over the sauce. Spread half the courgette mixture over the pasta, then sprinkle with some of the mozzarella and some of the Parmesan cheese. Repeat with more white sauce and another layer of lasagne, then cover with half the drained tomatoes.

Cover the tomatoes with lasagne, the remaining courgette mixture, and some mozzarella and Parmesan cheese. Repeat the layers ending with a layer of lasagne sheets, white sauce and the remaining Parmesan cheese. Bake in the preheated oven for 35 minutes, or until golden. Serve immediately.

Try this: FOR AN ALTERNATIVE: 136 FOR A LIGHT BITE: 46

Baked Macaroni Cheese

SERVES 8

450 g/1 lb macaroni
75 g/3 oz butter
1 onion, peeled and
    finely chopped
40 g/1½ oz plain flour
1 litre/1¾ pints milk
1–2 dried bay leaves
½ tsp dried thyme

salt and freshly ground
    black pepper
cayenne pepper
freshly grated nutmeg
2 small leeks, trimmed,
    finely chopped, cooked
    and drained
1 tbsp Dijon mustard

400 g/14 oz mature Cheddar
    cheese, grated
2 tbsp dried breadcrumbs
2 tbsp freshly grated
    Parmesan cheese
basil sprig, to garnish

Preheat the oven to 190°C/375°F/Gas Mark 5, 10 minutes before cooking. Bring a large pan of lightly salted water to a rolling boil. Add the macaroni and cook according to the packet instructions, or until 'al dente'. Drain thoroughly and reserve.

Meanwhile, melt 50 g/2 oz of the butter in a large, heavy-based saucepan, add the onion and cook, stirring frequently, for 5–7 minutes, or until softened. Sprinkle in the flour and cook, stirring constantly, for 2 minutes. Remove the pan from the heat, stir in the milk, return to the heat and cook, stirring, until a smooth sauce has formed. Add the bay leaf and thyme to the sauce and season to taste with salt, pepper, cayenne pepper and freshly grated nutmeg. Simmer for about 15 minutes, stirring frequently, until thickened and smooth.

Remove the sauce from the heat. Add the cooked leeks, mustard and Cheddar cheese and stir until the cheese has melted. Stir in the macaroni then tip into a lightly oiled baking dish.

Sprinkle the breadcrumbs and Parmesan cheese over the macaroni. Dot with the remaining butter, then bake in the preheated oven for 1 hour, or until golden. Garnish with a basil sprig and serve immediately.

Try this: FOR AN ALTERNATIVE: 276 FOR A LIGHT BITE: 50

Rigatoni with Gorgonzola & Walnuts

SERVES 4

400 g/14 oz rigatoni	double cream	Parmesan cheese
50 g/2 oz butter	75 g/3 oz walnut pieces,	salt and freshly ground
125 g/4 oz crumbled	lightly toasted and	black pepper
Gorgonzola cheese	coarsely chopped	cherry tomatoes, to serve
2 tbsp brandy, optional	1 tbsp freshly chopped basil	fresh green salad leaves,
200 ml/7 fl oz whipping or	50 g/2 oz freshly grated	to serve

Bring a large pan of lightly salted water to a rolling boil. Add the rigatoni and cook according to the packet instructions, or until 'al dente'. Drain the pasta thoroughly, reserve and keep warm.

Melt the butter in a large saucepan or wok over a medium heat. Add the Gorgonzola cheese and stir until just melted. Add the brandy if using and cook for 30 seconds, then pour in the cream and cook for 1–2 minutes, stirring until the sauce is smooth.

Stir in the walnut pieces, basil and half the Parmesan cheese, then add the rigatoni. Season to taste with salt and pepper. Return to the heat, stirring frequently, until heated through. Divide the pasta among 4 warmed pasta bowls, sprinkle with the remaining Parmesan cheese and serve immediately with cherry tomatoes and fresh green salad leaves.

Try this: FOR AN ALTERNATIVE: 312   FOR A LIGHT BITE: 58

Pumpkin–filled Pasta with Butter & Sage

SERVES 6-8

1 quantity fresh pasta dough
(see page 46)
125 g/4 oz butter
2 tbsp freshly shredded
sage leaves
50 g/2 oz freshly grated
Parmesan cheese,
to serve

For the filling:
250 g/9 oz freshly cooked
pumpkin or sweet potato
flesh, mashed and cooled
75–125 g/3–4 oz dried
breadcrumbs
125 g/4 oz freshly grated
Parmesan cheese

1 medium egg yolk
½ tsp soft brown sugar
2 tbsp freshly
chopped parsley
freshly grated nutmeg
salt and freshly ground
black pepper

Mix together the ingredients for the filling in a bowl, seasoning to taste with freshly grated nutmeg, salt and pepper. If the mixture seems too wet, add a few more breadcrumbs to bind.

Cut the pasta dough into quarters. Work with one quarter at a time, covering the remaining quarters with a damp tea towel. Roll out a quarter very thinly into a strip 10 cm/4 inches wide. Drop spoonfuls of the filling along the strip 6.5 cm/2½ inches apart, in 2 rows about 5 cm/2 inches apart. Moisten the outside edges and the spaces between the filling with water.

Roll out another strip of pasta and lay it over the filled strip. Press down gently along both edges and between the filled sections. Using a fluted pastry wheel, cut along both long sides, down the centre and between the fillings to form cushions. Transfer the cushions to a lightly floured baking sheet. Continue making cushions and allow to dry for 30 minutes.

Bring a large saucepan of slightly salted water to the boil. Add the pasta cushions and return to the boil. Cook, stirring frequently, for 4–5 minutes, or until 'al dente'. Drain carefully. Heat the butter in a pan, stir in the shredded sage leaves and cook for 30 seconds. Add the pasta cushions, stir gently then spoon into serving bowls. Sprinkle with the grated Parmesan cheese and serve immediately.

Try this: FOR AN ALTERNATIVE: 256 FOR A LIGHT BITE: 24

Tortellini, Cherry Tomato & Mozzarella Skewers

SERVES 6

250 g/9 oz mixed green
   and plain cheese or
   vegetable-filled
   fresh tortellini
150 ml/¼ pint extra virgin
   olive oil

2 garlic cloves, peeled
   and crushed
pinch dried thyme or basil
salt and freshly ground
   black pepper
225 g/8 oz cherry tomatoes

450 g/1 lb mozzarella, cut
   into 2.5 cm/1 inch cubes
basil leaves, to garnish
dressed salad leaves,
   to serve

Preheat the grill and line a grill pan with tinfoil, just before cooking. Bring a large pan of lightly salted water to a rolling boil. Add the tortellini and cook according to the packet instructions, or until 'al dente'. Drain, rinse under cold running water, drain again and toss with 2 tablespoons of the olive oil and reserve.

Pour the remaining olive oil into a small bowl. Add the crushed garlic and thyme or basil, then blend well. Season to taste with salt and black pepper and reserve.

To assemble the skewers, thread the tortellini alternately with the cherry tomatoes and cubes of mozzarella. Arrange the skewers on the grill pan and brush generously on all sides with the olive oil mixture.

Cook the skewers under the preheated grill for about 5 minutes, or until they begin to turn golden, turning them halfway through cooking. Arrange 2 skewers on each plate and garnish with a few basil leaves. Serve immediately with dressed salad leaves.

Tortellini & Summer Vegetable Salad

SERVES 6

350 g/12 oz mixed green and plain cheese-filled fresh tortellini
150 ml/¼ pint extra virgin olive oil
225 g/8 oz fine green beans, trimmed
175 g/6 oz broccoli florets
1 yellow or red pepper, deseeded and thinly sliced
1 red onion, peeled and sliced
175 g jar marinated artichoke hearts, drained and halved
2 tbsp capers
75 g/3 oz dry-cured pitted black olives
3 tbsp raspberry or balsamic vinegar
1 tbsp Dijon mustard
1 tsp soft brown sugar
salt and freshly ground black pepper
2 tbsp freshly chopped basil or flat-leaf parsley
2 quartered hard-boiled eggs, to garnish

Bring a large pan of lightly salted water to a rolling boil. Add the tortellini and cook according to the packet instructions, or until 'al dente'. Using a large slotted spoon, transfer the tortellini to a colander to drain. Rinse under cold running water and drain again. Transfer to a large bowl and toss with 2 tablespoons of the olive oil.

Return the pasta water to the boil and drop in the green beans and broccoli florets; blanch them for 2 minutes, or until just beginning to soften. Drain, rinse under cold running water and drain again thoroughly. Add the vegetables to the reserved tortellini. Add the pepper, onion, artichoke hearts, capers and olives to the bowl; stir lightly.

Whisk together the vinegar, mustard and brown sugar in a bowl and season to taste with salt and pepper. Slowly whisk in the remaining olive oil to form a thick, creamy dressing. Pour over the tortellini and vegetables, add the chopped basil or parsley and stir until lightly coated. Transfer to a shallow serving dish or salad bowl. Garnish with the hard-boiled egg quarters and serve.

Try this: FOR AN ALTERNATIVE: 266   FOR A LIGHT BITE: 56

Entertaining & Desserts

Tagliatelle with Stuffed Pork Escalopes

SERVES 4

150 g/5 oz broccoli
   florets, finely chopped
   and blanched
125 g/4 oz mozzarella
   cheese, grated
1 garlic clove, peeled
   and crushed

2 large eggs, beaten
   salt and freshly ground
   black pepper
4 thin pork escalopes,
   weighing about
   100 g/3½ oz each
1 tbsp olive oil

25 g/1 oz butter
2 tbsp flour
150 ml/¼ pint milk
150 ml/¼ pint chicken stock
1 tbsp Dijon mustard
225 g/8 oz fresh tagliatelle
sage leaves, to garnish

Preheat the oven to 180°C/350°F/Gas Mark 4, 10 minutes before cooking. Mix the broccoli with the mozzarella cheese, garlic and beaten eggs. Season to taste with salt and pepper and reserve.

Using a meat mallet or rolling pin, pound the escalopes on a sheet of greaseproof paper until 5 mm/¼ inch thick. Divide the broccoli mixture between the escalopes and roll each one up from the shortest side. Place the pork rolls in a lightly oiled ovenproof dish, drizzle over the olive oil and bake in the preheated oven for 40–50 minutes, or until cooked.

Meanwhile, melt the butter in a heavy-based pan, stir in the flour and cook for 2 minutes. Remove from the heat and whisk in the milk and stock. Season to taste, stir in the mustard then cook until smooth and thickened. Keep warm.

Bring a large pan of lightly salted water to a rolling boil. Add the taglietelle and cook according to the packet instructions, about 3–4 minutes, or until 'al dente'. Drain thoroughly and tip into a warmed serving dish. Slice each pork roll into 3, place on top of the pasta and pour the sauce over. Garnish with sage leaves and serve immediately.

Try this: FOR AN ALTERNATIVE: 192   FOR A LIGHT BITE: 26

Spicy Chicken with Open Ravioli & Tomato Sauce

SERVES 2-3

2 tbsp olive oil
1 onion, peeled and
    finely chopped
1 tsp ground cumin
1 tsp hot paprika pepper
1 tsp ground cinnamon
175 g/6 oz boneless and

skinless chicken
    breasts, chopped
salt and freshly ground
    black pepper
1 tbsp smooth peanut butter
50 g/2 oz butter
1 shallot, peeled and

finely chopped
2 garlic cloves, peeled
    and crushed
400 g can chopped tomatoes
125 g/4 oz fresh egg lasagne
2 tbsp freshly chopped
    coriander

Heat the olive oil in a frying pan, add the onion and cook gently for 2–3 minutes then add the cumin, paprika pepper and cinnamon and cook for a further 1 minute. Add the chicken, season to taste with salt and pepper and cook for 3–4 minutes, or until tender. Add the peanut butter and stir until well mixed and reserve.

Melt the butter in the frying pan, add the shallot and cook for 2 minutes. Add the tomatoes and garlic and season to taste. Simmer gently for 20 minutes, or until thickened, then keep the sauce warm.

Cut each sheet of lasagne into 6 squares. Bring a large pan of lightly salted water to a rolling boil. Add the lasagne squares and cook according to the packet instructions, about 3–4 minutes, or until 'al dente'. Drain the lasagne pieces thoroughly, reserve and keep warm.

Layer the pasta squares with the spicy filling on individual warmed plates. Pour over a little of the hot tomato sauce and sprinkle with chopped coriander. Serve immediately.

Try this: FOR AN ALTERNATIVE: 226 FOR A LIGHT BITE: 56

Farfalle & Chicken in White Wine Sauce

SERVES 4

4 boneless and skinless
   chicken breasts, about
      450 g/1 lb in total weight
salt and freshly ground
   black pepper
125 g/4 oz feta cheese
1 small egg, beaten

2 tbsp freshly chopped
   tarragon
50 g/2 oz butter
1 tbsp olive oil
1 onion, peeled and sliced
   into rings
150 ml/¼ pint white wine

150 ml/¼ pint chicken stock
350 g/12 oz fresh farfalle
3–4 tbsp soured cream
2 tbsp freshly chopped
   parsley

Place the chicken breasts between two sheets of greaseproof paper and, using a meat mallet or wooden rolling pin, pound as thinly as possible. Season with salt and pepper and reserve.

Mash the feta cheese with a fork and blend with the egg and half the tarragon. Divide the mixture between the chicken breasts and roll up each one. Secure with cocktail sticks.

Heat half the butter and all the olive oil in a frying pan, add the onion and cook for 2–3 minutes. Remove, using a slotted spoon, and reserve. Add the chicken parcels to the pan and cook for 3–4 minutes, or until browned. Pour in the wine and the stock and stir in the remaining tarragon. Cover and simmer gently for 10–15 minutes, or until the chicken is cooked.

Meanwhile, bring a large pan of lightly salted water to a rolling boil. Add the farfalle and cook according to the packet instructions, about 3–4 minutes, or until 'al dente'. Drain, toss in the remaining butter and tip into a warmed serving dish.

Slice each chicken roll into 4 and place on the pasta. Whisk the sauce until smooth, then stir in the soured cream and the reserved onions. Heat the sauce gently, then pour over the chicken. Sprinkle with the parsley and serve immediately.

Try this: FOR AN ALTERNATIVE: 188 FOR A LIGHT BITE: 18

Gnocchi Roulade
with Mozzarella & Spinach

SERVES 8

600 ml/1 pint milk
125 g/4 oz fine semolina
 or polenta
25 g/1 oz butter
75 g/3 oz Cheddar
 cheese, grated
2 medium egg yolks

salt and freshly ground
 black pepper
700 g/1½ lb baby spinach
 leaves
½ tsp freshly grated nutmeg
1 garlic clove, peeled
 and crushed

2 tbsp olive oil
150 g/5 oz mozzarella
 cheese, grated
2 tbsp freshly grated
 Parmesan cheese
freshly made tomato sauce,
 to serve

Preheat the oven to 240°C/475°F/Gas Mark 9, 15 minutes before cooking. Oil and line a large Swiss roll tin (23 cm/9 inch x 33 cm/13 inch) with non-stick baking parchment.

Pour the milk into a heavy-based pan and whisk in the semolina. Bring to the boil then simmer, stirring continuously with a wooden spoon, for 3–4 minutes, or until very thick. Remove from heat and stir in the butter and Cheddar cheese until melted. Whisk in the egg yolks and season to taste with salt and pepper. Pour into the lined tin. Cover and allow to cool for 1 hour.

Cook the baby spinach in batches in a large pan with 1 teaspoon of water for 3–4 minutes, or until wilted. Drain thoroughly, season to taste with salt, pepper and nutmeg, then allow to cool.

Spread the spinach over the cooled semolina mixture and sprinkle over 75 g/3 oz of the mozzarella and half the Parmesan cheese. Bake in the preheated oven for 20 minutes, or until golden.

Allow to cool, then roll up like a Swiss roll. Sprinkle with the remaining mozzarella and Parmesan cheese, then bake for another 15–20 minutes, or until golden. Serve immediately with freshly made tomato sauce.

Try this: FOR AN ALTERNATIVE: 168 FOR A LIGHT BITE: 50

Spaghetti with Smoked Salmon & Tiger Prawns

SERVES 4

225 g/8 oz baby spinach
  leaves
salt and freshly ground
  black pepper
pinch freshly grated nutmeg
225 g/8 oz cooked tiger
  prawns in their

shells, cooked
450 g/1 lb fresh angel
  hair spaghetti
50 g/2 oz butter
3 medium eggs
1 tbsp freshly chopped dill,
  plus extra to garnish

125 g/4 oz smoked salmon,
  cut into strips
dill sprigs, to garnish
2 tbsp grated Parmesan
  cheese, to serve

Cook the baby spinach leaves in a large pan with 1 teaspoon of water for 3–4 minutes, or until wilted. Drain thoroughly, season to taste with salt, pepper and nutmeg and keep warm. Remove the shells from all but 4 of the tiger prawns and reserve.

Bring a large pan of lightly salted water to a rolling boil. Add the pasta and cook according to the packet instructions, about 3–4 minutes, or until 'al dente'. Drain thoroughly and return to the pan. Stir in the butter and the peeled prawns, cover and keep warm.

Beat the eggs with the dill, season well, then stir into the spaghettini and prawns. Return the pan to the heat briefly, just long enough to lightly scramble the eggs, then remove from the heat. Carefully mix in the smoked salmon strips and the cooked spinach. Toss gently to mix. Tip into a warmed serving dish and garnish with the reserved prawns and dill sprigs. Serve immediately with grated Parmesan cheese.

Try this: FOR AN ALTERNATIVE: 112 FOR A LIGHT BITE: 42

Salmon & Mushroom Linguine

SERVES 4

450 g/1 lb salmon
    fillets, skinned
salt and freshly ground
    black pepper
75 g/3 oz butter
40 g/1½ oz flour

300 ml/½ pint chicken stock
150 ml/¼ pint whipping
    cream
225 g/8 oz mushrooms,
    wiped and sliced
350 g/12 oz linguine

50 g/2 oz Cheddar
    cheese, grated
50 g/2 oz fresh white
    breadcrumbs
2 tbsp freshly chopped
    parsley, to garnish

Preheat the oven to 190°C/375°F/Gas Mark 5, 10 minutes before cooking. Place the salmon in a shallow pan and cover with water. Season well with salt and pepper and bring to the boil, then lower the heat and simmer for 6–8 minutes, or until cooked. Drain and keep warm.

Melt 50 g/2 oz of the butter in a heavy-based pan, stir in the flour, cook for 1 minute then whisk in the chicken stock. Simmer gently until thickened. Stir in the cream and season to taste. Keep the sauce warm.

Melt the remaining butter, in a pan, add the sliced mushrooms and cook for 2–3 minutes. Stir the mushrooms into the white sauce.

Bring a large pan of lightly salted water to a rolling boil. Add the linguine and cook according to the packet instructions, or until 'al dente'.

Drain the pasta thoroughly and return to the pan. Stir in half the sauce, then spoon into a lightly oiled a 1.4 litre/2½ pint shallow ovenproof dish. Flake the salmon, add to the remaining sauce then pour over the pasta. Sprinkle with the cheese and breadcrumbs, then bake in the preheated for 15–20 minutes, or until golden. Garnish with the parsley and serve immediately.

Try this: FOR AN ALTERNATIVE: 302 FOR A LIGHT BITE: 64

Spaghetti with Hot Chilli Mussels

SERVES 4

900 g/2 lb fresh live mussels
300 ml/½ pint white wine
3–4 garlic cloves, peeled
   and crushed
2 tbsp olive oil

1–2 bird's-eye chillies,
   deseeded and chopped
2 x 400 g cans chopped
   tomatoes
salt and freshly ground

    black pepper
350 g/12 oz fresh spaghetti
2 tbsp freshly chopped
   parsley, to garnish
warm crusty bread, to serve

Scrub the mussels and remove any beards. Discard any that do not close when tapped. Place in a large pan with the white wine and half the crushed garlic. Cover and cook over a high heat for 5–6 minutes, shaking the pan from time to time. When the mussels have opened, drain, reserving the juices and straining them through a muslin-lined sieve. Discard any mussels that have not opened and keep the rest warm.

Heat the oil in a heavy-based pan, add the remaining garlic with the chillies and cook for 30 seconds. Stir in the chopped tomatoes and 75 ml/3 fl oz of the reserved cooking liquor and simmer for 15–20 minutes. Season to taste with salt and pepper.

Meanwhile, bring a large pan of lightly salted water to a rolling boil. Add the spaghetti and cook according to the packet instructions, about 3–4 minutes, or until 'al dente'.

Drain the spaghetti thoroughly and return to the pan. Add the mussels and tomato sauce to the pasta, toss lightly to cover, then tip into a warmed serving dish or spoon on to individual plates. Garnish with chopped parsley and serve immediately with warm crusty bread.

Pasta Triangles with Pesto & Walnut Dressing

SERVES 6

450 g/1 lb fresh egg lasagne
4 tbsp ricotta cheese
4 tbsp pesto
125 g/4 oz walnuts
1 slice white bread,
   crusts removed
150 ml/¼ pint soured cream

75 g/3 oz mascarpone
   cheese
25 g/1 oz pecorino
   cheese, grated
salt and freshly ground
   black pepper
1 tbsp olive oil

sprig of dill or freshly
   chopped basil or parsley,
   to garnish
tomato and cucumber salad,
   to serve

Preheat the grill to high. Cut the lasagne sheets in half, then into triangles and reserve. Mix the pesto and ricotta cheese together and warm gently in a pan.

Toast the walnuts under the preheated grill until golden. Rub off the papery skins. Place the nuts in a food processor with the bread and grind finely.

Mix the soured cream with the mascarpone cheese in a bowl. Add the ground walnuts and grated pecorino cheese and season to taste with salt and pepper. Whisk in the olive oil. Pour into a pan and warm gently.

Bring a large pan of lightly salted water to a rolling boil. Add the pasta triangles and cook, according to the packet instructions, about 3–4 minutes, or until 'al dente'.

Drain the pasta thoroughly and arrange a few triangles on each serving plate. Top each one with a spoonful of the pesto mixture then place another triangle on top. Continue to layer the pasta and pesto mixture, then spoon a little of the walnut sauce on top of each stack. Garnish with dill, basil or parsley and serve immediately with a freshly dressed tomato and cucumber salad.

Try this: FOR AN ALTERNATIVE: 274 FOR A LIGHT BITE: 58

Aubergine & Tomato Layer

SERVES 4

2 aubergines, about
   700 g/1½ lb, trimmed
   and thinly sliced
6 tbsp olive oil
1 onion, peeled and
   finely sliced
1 garlic clove, peeled
   and crushed

400 g can chopped tomatoes
50 ml/2 fl oz red wine
½ tsp sugar
salt and freshly ground
   black pepper
50 g/2 oz butter
40 g/1½ oz flour
450 ml/¾ pint milk

225 g/8 oz fresh egg lasagne
2 medium eggs, beaten
200 ml/7 fl oz Greek yogurt
125 g/3 oz mozzarella
   cheese, grated
fresh basil leaves, to garnish

Preheat the oven to 190°C/375°F/Gas Mark 5, 10 minutes before cooking. Brush the aubergine slices with 5 tablespoons of the olive oil and place on a baking sheet. Bake in the preheated oven for 20 minutes, or until tender. Remove from the oven and increase the temperature to 200°C/400°F/Gas Mark 6.

Heat the remaining oil in a heavy-based pan. Add the onion and garlic, cook for 2–3 minutes then add the tomatoes, wine and sugar. Season to taste with salt and pepper, then simmer for 20 minutes.

Melt the butter in another pan. Stir in the flour, cook for 2 minutes, then whisk in the milk. Cook for 2–3 minutes, or until thickened. Season to taste.

Pour a little white sauce into a lightly oiled, 1.7 litre/3 pint baking dish. Cover with a layer of lasagne, spread with tomato sauce, then add some of the aubergines. Cover thinly with white sauce and sprinkle with a little cheese. Continue to layer in this way, finishing with a layer of lasagne.

Beat together the eggs and yogurt. Season, then pour over the lasagne. Sprinkle with the remaining cheese and bake in the preheated oven for 25–30 minutes, or until golden. Garnish with basil leaves and serve.

Try this: FOR AN ALTERNATIVE: 280   FOR A LIGHT BITE: 36

Cannelloni with Gorgonzola Sauce

SERVES 2-3

50 g/2 oz salted butter
1 shallot, peeled and
  finely chopped
2 rashers streaky bacon, rind
  removed and chopped
225 g/8 oz mushrooms,

wiped and finely chopped
25 g/1 oz plain flour
120 ml/4 fl oz double cream
125 g/4 oz fresh egg lasagne,
  6 sheets in total
40 g/1½ oz unsalted butter

150 g/5 oz Gorgonzola
  cheese, diced
150 ml/¼ pint whipping
  cream
assorted salad leaves,
  to serve

Preheat the oven to 190°C/375°F/Gas Mark 5, 10 minutes before cooking. Melt the salted butter in a heavy-based pan, add the shallot and bacon and cook for about 4–5 minutes.

Add the mushrooms to the pan and cook for 5–6 minutes, or until the mushrooms are very soft. Stir in the flour, cook for 1 minute, then stir in the double cream and cook gently for 2 minutes. Allow to cool.

Cut each sheet of lasagne in half. Spoon some filling on to each piece and roll up from the longest side to resemble cannelloni. Arrange the cannelloni in a lightly oiled, shallow 1.4 litre/2½ pint ovenproof dish.

Heat the unsalted butter very slowly in a pan and when melted, add the Gorgonzola cheese. Stir until the cheese has melted, then stir in the whipping cream. Bring to the boil slowly, then simmer gently for about 5 minutes, or until thickened.

Pour the cream sauce over the cannelloni. Place in the preheated oven and bake for 20 minutes, or until golden and thoroughly heated through. Serve immediately with assorted salad leaves.

Try this: FOR AN ALTERNATIVE: 284 FOR A LIGHT BITE: 58

Lamb & Pasta Pie

SERVES 8

400 g/14 oz plain white flour
100 g/3½ oz margarine
100 g/3½ oz white
   vegetable fat
pinch of salt
1 small egg, separated
50 g/2 oz butter
50 g/2 oz flour

450 ml/¾ pint milk
salt and freshly ground
   black pepper
225 g/8 oz macaroni
50 g/2 oz Cheddar
   cheese, grated
1 tbsp vegetable oil
1 onion, peeled and chopped

1 garlic clove, peeled and
   crushed
2 celery sticks, trimmed and
   chopped
450 g/1 lb lamb mince
1 tbsp tomato paste
400 g can chopped tomatoes

Preheat the oven to 190°C/375°F/Gas Mark 5, 10 minutes before cooking. Lightly oil a 20.5 cm/ 8 inch spring-form cake tin. Blend the flour, salt, margarine and white vegetable fat in a food processor and add cold water to make a smooth, pliable dough. Knead on a lightly floured surface, then roll out two-thirds to line the base and sides of the tin. Brush with egg white and reserve.

Melt the butter in a heavy-based pan, stir in the flour and cook for 2 minutes. Stir in the milk and cook, stirring, until a smooth, thick sauce is formed. Season to taste with salt and pepper and reserve. Bring a large pan of lightly salted water to a rolling boil. Add the macaroni and cook according to the packet instructions, or until *al dente*. Drain, then stir into the white sauce with the grated cheese. Heat the oil in a frying pan, add the onion, garlic, celery and lamb mince and cook, stirring, for 5–6 minutes. Stir in the tomato paste and tomatoes and cook for 10 minutes. Cool slightly.

Place half the pasta mixture, then all the mince in the pastry-lined tin. Top with a layer of pasta. Roll out the remaining pastry and cut out a lid. Brush the edge with water, place over the filling and pinch the edges together. Use trimmings to decorate the top of the pie. Brush the pie with beaten egg yolk and bake in the preheated oven for 50–60 minutes, covering the top with tin- foil if browning too quickly. Stand for 15 minutes before turning out. Serve immediately.

Try this: FOR AN ALTERNATIVE: 166 FOR A LIGHT BITE: 22

Baked Macaroni with Mushrooms & Leeks

SERVES 4

2 tbsp olive oil
1 onion, peeled and finely chopped
1 garlic clove, peeled and crushed
2 small leeks, trimmed and chopped

450 g/1 lb assorted wild mushrooms, trimmed
50 ml/2 fl oz white wine
75 g/3 oz butter
150 ml/¼ pint crème fraîche or whipping cream
salt and freshly ground

black pepper
75 g/3 oz fresh white breadcrumbs
350 g/12 oz short cut macaroni
1 tbsp freshly chopped parsley, to garnish

Preheat the oven to 220°C/425°F/Gas Mark 7, 15 minutes before cooking. Heat 1 tablespoon of the olive oil in a large frying pan, add the onion and garlic and cook for 2 minutes. Add the leeks, mushrooms and 25 g/1 oz of the butter then cook for 5 minutes. Pour in the white wine, cook for 2 minutes then stir in the crème fraîche or cream. Season to taste with salt and pepper.

Meanwhile, bring a large pan of lightly salted water to a rolling boil. Add the macaroni and cook according to the packet instructions, or until 'al dente'.

Melt 25 g/1 oz of the butter with the remaining oil in a small frying pan. Add the breadcrumbs and fry until just beginning to turn golden-brown. Drain on absorbent kitchen paper.

Drain the pasta thoroughly, toss in the remaining butter then tip into a lightly oiled, 1.4 litre/2½ pint shallow baking dish. Cover the pasta with the leek and mushroom mixture then sprinkle with the fried breadcrumbs. Bake in the preheated oven for 5–10 minutes, or until golden and crisp. Garnish with chopped parsley and serve.

Try this: FOR AN ALTERNATIVE: 282   FOR A LIGHT BITE: 66

Vanilla & Lemon Panna Cotta with Raspberry Sauce

SERVES 6

900 ml/1½ pints double cream	zest of 1 lemon	3–4 tbsp icing sugar, to taste
1 vanilla pod, split	3 sheets gelatine	1 tbsp lemon juice
100 g/3½ oz caster sugar	5 tbsp milk	extra lemon zest, to decorate
	450 g/1 lb raspberries	

Put the cream, vanilla pod and sugar into a saucepan. Bring to the boil, then simmer for 10 minutes until slightly reduced, stirring to prevent scalding. Remove from the heat, stir in the lemon zest and remove the vanilla pod.

Soak the gelatine in the milk for 5 minutes, or until softened. Squeeze out any excess milk and add to the hot cream. Stir well until dissolved.

Pour the cream mixture into 6 ramekins or mini pudding moulds and leave in the refrigerator for 4 hours, or until set.

Meanwhile, put 175 g/6 oz of the raspberries in a food processor with the icing sugar and lemon juice. Blend to a purée then pass the mixture through a sieve. Fold in the remaining raspberries with a metal spoon or rubber spatula and chill in the refrigerator until ready to serve.

To serve, dip each of the moulds into hot water for a few seconds, then turn out on to 6 individual serving plates. Spoon some of the raspberry sauce over and around the panna cotta, decorate with extra lemon zest and serve.

Try this: FOR AN ALTERNATIVE: 348 FOR A MAIN MEAL: 130

Ricotta Cheesecake with Strawberry Coulis

SERVES 6-8

125 g/4 oz digestive biscuits
100 g/3½ oz candied
   peel, chopped
65 g/2½ oz butter, melted
150 ml/¼ pint crème fraîche

575 g/4 oz ricotta cheese
100 g/3½ oz caster sugar
1 vanilla pod, seeds only
2 large eggs
225 g/8 oz strawberries

25–50 g/1–2 oz caster sugar,
   to taste
zest and juice of 1 orange

Preheat oven to 170°C/325°F/Gas Mark 3. Line a 20.5 cm/8 inch springform tin with baking parchment. Place the biscuits into a food processor together with the peel. Blend until the biscuits are crushed and the peel is chopped. Add 50 g/2 oz of the melted butter and process until mixed. Tip into the tin and spread evenly over the bottom. Press firmly into place and reserve.

Blend together the crème fraîche, ricotta cheese, sugar, vanilla seeds and eggs in a food processor. With the motor running, add the remaining melted butter and blend for a few seconds. Pour the mixture on to the base. Transfer to the preheated oven and cook for about 1 hour, until set and risen round the edges, but slightly wobbly in the centre. Switch off the oven and allow to cool there. chill in the refrigerator for at least 8 hours, or preferably overnight.

Wash and drain the strawberries. Hull the fruit and remove any soft spots. Put into the food processor along with 25 g/1 oz of the sugar and orange juice and zest. Blend until smooth. Add the remaining sugar to taste. Pass through a sieve to remove seeds and chill in the refrigerator until needed.

Cut the cheesecake into wedges, spoon over some of the strawberry coulis and serve.

Cantuccini

MAKES 24 BISCUITS

250 g/9 oz plain flour
250 g/9 oz caster sugar
½ tsp baking powder
½ tsp vanilla essence
2 medium eggs

1 medium egg yolk
100 g/3½ oz mixed almonds
   and hazelnuts, toasted
   and roughly chopped
1 tsp whole aniseed

1 medium egg yolk
   mixed with
1 tbsp water, to glaze
Vin Santo or coffee, to serve

Preheat oven to 180°C/350°F/Gas Mark 4. Line a large baking sheet with non-stick baking parchment. Place the flour, caster sugar, baking powder, vanilla essence, the whole eggs and one of the egg yolks into a food processor and blend until the mixture forms a ball, scraping down the sides once or twice. Turn the mixture out on to a lightly floured surface and knead in the chopped nuts and aniseed.

Divide the paste into 3 pieces and roll into logs about 4 cm/1½ inches wide. Place the logs on to the baking sheet at least 5 cm/2 inches apart. Brush lightly with the other egg yolk beaten with 1 tablespoon of water and bake in the preheated oven for 30–35 minutes.

Remove from the oven and reduce the oven temperature to 150°C/300°F/Gas Mark 2. Cut the logs diagonally into 2.5 cm/1 inch slices and lay cut-side down on the baking sheet. Return to the oven for a further 30–40 minutes, or until dry and firm. Cool on a wire rack and store in an airtight container. Serve with Vin Santo or coffee.

Try this: FOR AN ALTERNATIVE: 326 FOR A MAIN MEAL: 178

Almond & Pistachio Biscotti

MAKES 12 BISCUITS

125 g/4 oz ground almonds
50 g/2 oz shelled pistachios
50 g/2 oz blanched almonds
2 medium eggs

1 medium egg yolk
125 g/4 oz icing sugar
225 g/8 oz plain flour
1 tsp baking powder

pinch of salt
zest of ½ lemon

Preheat oven to 180°C/350°F/Gas Mark 4. Line a large baking sheet with non-stick baking parchment. Toast the ground almonds and whole nuts lightly and reserve until cool.

Beat together the eggs, egg yolk and icing sugar until thick, then beat in the flour, baking powder and salt. Add the lemon zest, ground almonds and whole nuts and mix to form a slightly sticky dough.

Turn the dough on to a lightly floured surface and, using lightly floured hands, form into a log measuring approximately 30 cm/12 inches long. Place down the centre of the prepared baking sheet and transfer to the preheated oven. Bake for 20 minutes.

Remove from the oven and increase the oven temperature to 200°C/400°F/Gas Mark 6. Cut the log diagonally into 2.5 cm/1 inch slices. Return to the baking sheet, cut-side down and bake for a further 10–15 minutes until golden, turning once after 10 minutes. Leave to cool on a wire rack and store in an airtight container.

Try this: FOR AN ALTERNATIVE: 340   FOR A MAIN MEAL: 234

Hazelnut, Chocolate & Chestnut Meringue Torte

SERVES 8–10

For the chocolate meringue:
1 medium egg white
50 g/2 oz caster sugar
2 tbsp cocoa powder

For the hazelnut meringue:
75 g/3 oz hazelnuts, toasted

2 medium egg whites
125 g/4 oz caster sugar

For the filling:
300 ml/½ pint double cream
250 g can sweetened
    chestnut purée

50 g/2 oz plain dark
    chocolate, melted
25 g/1 oz plain dark
    chocolate, grated

Preheat oven to 130°C/250°F/Gas Mark 1⁄2. Line 3 baking sheets with non-stick baking parchment and draw a 20.5 cm/8 inch circle on each. Beat 1 egg white until stiff peaks form. Add 25 g/1 oz of the sugar and beat until shiny. Mix the cocoa with the remaining 25 g/1 oz of sugar and add 1 tablespoon at a time, beating well after each addition, until all the sugar is added and the mixture is stiff and glossy. Spread on to 1 of the baking sheets within the circle drawn on the underside.

Put the hazelnuts in a food processor and blend until chopped. In a clean bowl, beat the 2 egg whites until stiff. Add 50 g/2 oz of the sugar and beat. Add the remaining sugar about 1 tablespoon at a time, beating after each addition until all the sugar is added and the mixture is stiff and glossy. Reserve 2 tablespoons of the nuts, then fold in the remainder and divide between the 2 remaining baking sheets. Sprinkle one of the hazelnut meringues with the reserved hazelnuts and transfer all the baking sheets to the oven. Bake in the preheated oven for 1½ hours. Turn the oven off and leave in the oven until cold.

Whip the cream until thick. Beat the chestnut purée in another bowl until soft. Add a spoonful of the cream and fold together before adding the remaining cream and melted chocolate and fold together. Place the plain hazelnut meringue on a serving plate. Top with half the cream and chestnut mixture. Add the chocolate meringue and top with the remaining cream. Add the final meringue. Sprinkle over the grated chocolate and serve.

Try this: FOR AN ALTERNATIVE: 336 FOR A MAIN MEAL: 224

Bomba Siciliana

SERVES 6–8

100 g/3½ oz plain chocolate,
    broken into pieces
200 g/7 oz fresh chilled
    custard
150 ml/¼ pint whipping
    cream

25 g/1 oz candied peel,
    finely chopped
25 g/1 oz glacé cherries,
    chopped
25 g/1 oz sultanas
3 tbsp rum

225 g/8 oz good-quality
    vanilla ice cream
200 ml/¼ pint double cream
3 tbsp caster sugar

Melt the plain chocolate in bowl set over a saucepan of simmering water until smooth, then cool. Whisk together the custard with the whipping cream and slightly cooled chocolate Spoon the mixture into a shallow, lidded freezer box and freeze. Every 2 hours, remove from the freezer and using an electric whisk or balloon whisk, whisk thoroughly. Repeat 3 times, then leave until frozen solid. Soak the candied peel, cherries and sultanas in the rum and leave until needed.

Chill a bombe or 1 litre/1¾ pint pudding mould in the freezer for about 30 minutes. Remove the chocolate ice cream from the freezer to soften, then spoon the ice cream into the mould and press down well, smoothing around the edges and leaving a hollow in the centre. Return the ice cream to the freezer for about 1 hour, or until frozen hard.

Remove the vanilla ice cream from the freezer to soften. Spoon the softened vanilla ice cream into the hollow, making sure to leave another hollow for the cream. Return to the freezer again and freeze until hard. Whip the cream and sugar until it is just holding its shape then fold in the soaked fruit. Remove the mould from the freezer and spoon in the cream mixture. Return to the freezer for at least another hour.

When ready to serve, remove the mould from the freezer and dip into hot water for a few seconds, then turn on to a large serving plate. Dip a knife into hot water and cut into wedges to serve.

Summer Fruit Semifreddo

SERVES 6–8

225 g/8 oz raspberries
125 g/4 oz blueberries
125 g/4 oz redcurrants
50 g/2 oz icing sugar

juice of 1 lemon
1 vanilla pod, split
50 g/2 oz sugar
4 large eggs, separated

600 ml/1 pint double cream
pinch of salt
fresh redcurrants,
   to decorate

Wash and hull or remove stalks from the fruits, as necessary, then put them into a food processor or blender with the icing sugar and lemon juice. Blend to a purée, pour into a jug and chill in the refrigerator, until needed.

Remove the seeds from the vanilla pod by opening the pod and scraping with the back of a knife. Add the seeds to the sugar and whisk with the egg yolks until pale and thick.

In another bowl, whip the cream until soft peaks form. Do not overwhip. In a third bowl, whip the egg whites with the salt until stiff peaks form.

Using a large metal spoon – to avoid knocking any air from the mixture – fold together the fruit purée, egg yolk mixture, the cream and egg whites. Transfer the mixture to a round, shallow, lidded freezer box and put into the freezer until almost frozen. If the mixture freezes solid, thaw in the refrigerator until semi-frozen. Turn out the semi-frozen mixture, cut into wedges and serve decorated with a few fresh redcurrants. If the mixture thaws completely, eat immediately and do not refreeze.

Try this: FOR AN ALTERNATIVE: 348   FOR A MAIN MEAL: 266

Cassatta

SERVES 6–8

300 g/11 oz plain chocolate, broken into pieces
200 g/7 oz fresh chilled custard
150 ml/¼ pint whipping cream

275 g/10 oz good-quality pistachio ice cream
25 g/1 oz shelled pistachios, toasted
50 g/2 oz candied peel, finely chopped

25 g/1 oz glacé cherries, finely chopped
275 g/10 oz good-quality strawberry ice cream

Line a 450 g/1 lb loaf tin with clingfilm. Place in the freezer. Melt 100 g/3½ oz of the chocolate into a heatproof bowl set over a saucepan of simmering water, stir until smooth, then cool. Place the custard into a bowl. Stir in the cream and the chocolate and stir until mixed. Spoon into a shallow, lidded freezer box and transfer to the freezer. Every 2 hours remove from the freezer and using an electric whisk, whisk thoroughly. Repeat 3 times, then leave until frozen solid.

Remove the chocolate ice cream from the freezer and allow to soften. Remove the loaf tin from the freezer and press the chocolate ice cream into the bottom of the tin, press down well and allow it to come up the sides of the tin. Return to the freezer and leave until solid.

Soften the pistachio ice cream, then beat in the pistachios, candied peel and cherries. Spoon into the tin, pressing down well and smoothing the top. Return to the freezer until hard. Soften the strawberry ice cream and spread on to the pistachio ice cream. Smooth the top. Return to the freezer for at least 1 hour, or until completely solid.

Meanwhile, melt the remaining chocolate, stir until smooth and cool slightly. Remove the loaf tin from the freezer. Dip into hot water and turn on to a serving dish. Using a teaspoon, drizzle the chocolate over the ice cream in a haphazard pattern. Return the cassatta to the freezer, until the chocolate has set. Dip a knife in hot water and use to slice the cassatta. Serve immediately.

Try this: FOR AN ALTERNATIVE: 330 FOR A MAIN MEAL: 274

Chestnut Cake

SERVES 8-10

175 g/6 oz butter, softened
175 g/6 oz caster sugar
250 g can sweetened
    chestnut purée
3 medium eggs,
    lightly beaten

175 g/6 oz plain flour
1 tsp baking powder
pinch of ground cloves
1 tsp fennel seeds, crushed
75 g/3 oz raisins
50 g/2 oz pine nuts, toasted

125 g/4 oz icing sugar
5 tbsp lemons juice
pared strips of lemon rind,
    to decorate

Preheat oven to 150°C/300°F/Gas Mark 2. Oil and line a 23 cm/9 inch springform tin. Beat together the butter and sugar until light and fluffy. Add the chestnut purée and beat. Gradually add the eggs, beating after each addition. Sift in the flour with the baking powder and cloves. Add the fennel seeds and beat. The mixture should drop easily from a wooden spoon when tapped against the side of the bowl. If not, add a little milk.

Beat in the raisins and pine nuts. Spoon the mixture into the prepared tin and smooth the top. Transfer to the centre of the oven and bake in the preheated oven for 55–60 minutes, or until a skewer inserted in the centre of the cake comes out clean. Remove from the oven and leave in the tin.

Meanwhile, mix together the icing sugar and lemon juice in a small saucepan until smooth. Heat gently until hot, but not boiling. Using a cocktail stick or skewer, poke holes into the cake all over. Pour the hot syrup evenly over the cake and leave to soak into the cake. Decorate with pared strips of lemon and serve.

Try this: FOR AN ALTERNATIVE: 328 FOR A MAIN MEAL: 122

Sauternes & Olive Oil Cake

SERVES 8-10

125 g/4 oz plain flour, plus
    extra for dusting
4 medium eggs
125 g/4 oz caster sugar
grated zest of ½ lemon

grated zest of ½ orange
2 tbsp Sauternes or other
    sweet dessert wine
3 tbsp very best quality
    extra-virgin olive oil

4 ripe peaches
1–2 tsp soft brown sugar,
    or to taste
1 tbsp lemon juice
icing sugar, to dust

Preheat oven to 140°C/275°F/Gas Mark 1. Oil and line a 25.5 cm/10 inch springform tin. Sift the flour on to a large sheet of greaseproof paper and reserve. Using a freestanding electric mixer, if possible, whisk the eggs and sugar together, until pale and stiff. Add the lemon and orange zest.

Turn the speed to low and pour the flour from the paper in a slow, steady stream on to the eggs and sugar mixture. Immediately add the wine and olive oil and switch the machine off as the olive oil should not be incorporated completely.

Using a rubber spatula, fold the mixture very gently 3 or 4 times so that the ingredients are just incorporated. Pour the mixture immediately into the prepared tin and bake in the preheated oven for 20–25 minutes, without opening the door for at least 15 minutes. Test if cooked by pressing the top lightly with a clean finger – if it springs back, remove from the oven, if not, bake for a little longer.

Leave the cake to cool in the tin on a wire rack. Remove the cake from the tin when cool enough to handle.

Meanwhile, skin the peaches and cut into segments. Toss with the brown sugar and lemon juice and reserve. When the cake is cold, dust generously with icing sugar, cut into wedges and serve with the peaches.

Try this: FOR AN ALTERNATIVE: 334   FOR A MAIN MEAL: 138

Frozen Amaretti Soufflé with Strawberries

SERVES 6-8

125 g/4 oz Amaretti biscuits
9 tbsp Amaretto liqueur
grated zest and juice of
   1 lemon
1 tbsp powdered gelatine

6 medium eggs, separated
175 g/6 oz soft brown sugar
600 ml/1 pint double cream
450 g/1 lb fresh strawberries,
   halved if large

1 vanilla pod, split and seeds
   scraped out
2 tbsp caster sugar
few finely crushed Amaretti
   biscuits, to decorate

Wrap a collar of greaseproof paper around a 900 ml/1½ pint soufflé dish or 6–8 individual ramekin dishes to extend at least 5 cm/2 inch above the rim and secure with string. Break the biscuits into a bowl. Sprinkle over 6 tablespoons of the Amaretto liqueur and leave to soak.

Put the lemon zest and juice into a small heatproof bowl and sprinkle over the gelatine. Leave for 5 minutes to sponge, then put the bowl over a saucepan of simmering water, ensuring that the base of the bowl does not touch the water. Stir occasionally until the gelatine has dissolved completely.

In a clean bowl, whisk the egg yolks and sugar until pale and thick then stir in the gelatine and the soaked biscuits. In another bowl, lightly whip 450 ml/¾ pint of the cream and using a large metal spoon or rubber spatula fold into the mixture. In a third clean bowl, whisk the egg whites until stiff, then fold into the soufflé mixture. Transfer to the prepared dish, or individual ramekin dishes, and level the top. Freeze for at least 8 hours, or preferably overnight.

Put the strawberries into a bowl with the vanilla pod and seeds, sugar and remaining Amaretto liqueur. Leave overnight in the refrigerator, then allow to come to room temperature before serving.

Place the soufflé in the refrigerator for about 1 hour. Whip the remaining cream and use to decorate the soufflé then sprinkle a few finely crushed Amaretti biscuits on the top and serve with the strawberries.

Almond & Pine Nut Tart

SERVES 6

250 g/9 oz ready-made
   sweet shortcrust pastry
75 g/3 oz blanched almonds
75 g/3 oz caster sugar
pinch of salt
2 medium eggs

1 tsp vanilla essence
2–3 drops almond essence
125 g/4 oz unsalted butter,
   softened
2 tbsp flour
½ tsp baking powder

3–4 tbsp raspberry jam
50 g/2 oz pine nuts
icing sugar, to decorate
whipped cream, to serve

Preheat oven to 200°C/400°F/Gas Mark 6. Roll out the pastry and use to line a 23 cm/9 inch fluted flan tin. Chill in the refrigerator for 10 minutes, then line with greaseproof paper and baking beans and bake blind in the preheated oven for 10 minutes. Remove the paper and beans and bake for a further 10–12 minutes until cooked. Leave to cool. Reduce the temperature to 190°C/375°F/Gas Mark 5.

Grind the almonds in a food processor until fine. Add the sugar, salt, eggs, vanilla and almond essence and blend. Add the butter, flour and baking powder and blend until smooth.

Spread a thick layer of the raspberry jam over the cooled pastry case, then pour in the almond filling. Sprinkle the pine nuts evenly over the top and bake for 30 minutes, until firm and browned.

Remove the tart from the oven and leave to cool. Dust generously with icing sugar and serve cut into wedges with whipped cream.

Try this: FOR AN ALTERNATIVE: 334 FOR A MAIN MEAL: 132

Coffee Ricotta

SERVES 6

700 g/1½ lb fresh
  ricotta cheese
125 ml/4 fl oz double cream
25 g/1 oz espresso beans,

freshly ground
4 tbsp caster sugar
3 tbsp brandy
50 g/2 oz butter, softened

75 g/3 oz caster sugar
1 medium egg, beaten
50 g/2 oz plain flour

Preheat oven to 220°C/425°F/Gas Mark 7, 15 minutes before baking. Beat the ricotta and cream together until smooth. Stir in the ground coffee beans, sugar and brandy. Cover and refrigerate for at least 2 hours (the flavour improves the longer it stands). Meanwhile, oil 2 baking sheets and line with non-stick baking parchment.

Cream together the butter and sugar until fluffy. Gradually beat in the egg, a little at a time. In a bowl, sift the flour then fold into the butter mixture to form a soft dough. Spoon the mixture into a piping bag fitted with a 1 cm/½ inch plain nozzle. Pipe 7.5 cm/3 inch lengths of the mixture spaced well apart on to the baking sheet. Use a sharp knife to cut the dough off cleanly at the nozzle.

Bake in the preheated oven for 6–8 minutes, until just golden at the edges. Cool on the baking sheet for 5 minutes before transferring to a wire rack to cool completely.

To serve, spoon the coffee and ricotta mixture into small coffee cups. Serve with the biscuits.

Try this: FOR AN ALTERNATIVE: 344 FOR A MAIN MEAL: 140

Zabaglione with Rum–soaked Raisin Compote

SERVES 6

2 tbsp raisins
1 strip thinly pared
  lemon zest
½ tsp ground cinnamon

3 tbsp Marsala wine
3 medium egg yolks
3 tbsp caster sugar
125 ml/4 fl oz dry white wine

150 ml/¼ pint double cream,
  lightly whipped
crisp biscuits, to serve

Put the raisins in a small bowl with the lemon zest and ground cinnamon. Pour over the Marsala wine to cover and leave to macerate for at least one hour. When the raisins are plump, lift out of the Marsala wine and reserve the raisins and wine, discarding the lemon zest.

In a large heatproof bowl, mix together the egg yolks and sugar. Add the white wine and Marsala wine and stir well to combine. Put the bowl over a saucepan of simmering water, ensuring that the bottom of the bowl does not touch the water. Whisk constantly until the mixture doubles in bulk.

Remove from the heat and continue whisking for about 5 minutes until the mixture has cooled slightly. Fold in the raisins and then immediately fold in the whipped cream. Spoon into dessert glasses or goblets and serve with crisp biscuits.

Try this: FOR AN ALTERNATIVE: 334 FOR A MAIN MEAL: 298

Goats' Cheese & Lemon Tart

SERVES 8-10

For the pastry:
125 g/4 oz butter, cut into small pieces
225 g/8 oz plain flour
pinch of salt
50 g/2 oz caster sugar

1 medium egg yolk

For the filling:
350 g/12 oz mild fresh goats' cheese, eg Chavroux
3 medium eggs, beaten

150 g/5 oz caster sugar
grated rind and juice of 3 lemons
450 ml/¾ pint double cream
fresh raspberries, to decorate and serve

Preheat oven to 200°C/400°F/Gas Mark 6, 15 minutes before cooking. Rub the butter into the plain flour and salt until the mixture resembles breadcrumbs, then stir in the sugar. Beat the egg yolk with 2 tablespoons of cold water and add to the mixture. Mix together until a dough is formed then turn the dough out on to a lightly floured surface and knead until smooth. Chill in the refrigerator for 30 minutes.

Roll the dough out thinly on a lightly floured surface and use to line a 4 cm/1½ inch deep 23 cm/9 inch fluted flan tin. Chill in the refrigerator for 10 minutes. Line the pastry case with greaseproof paper and baking beans or tinfoil and bake blind in the preheated oven for 10 minutes. Remove the paper and beans or tinfoil. Return to the oven for a further 12–15 minutes until cooked. Leave to cool slightly, then reduce the oven temperature to 150°C/300°F/Gas Mark 2.

Beat the goats' cheese until smooth. Whisk in the eggs, sugar, lemon rind and juice. Add the cream and mix well.

Carefully pour the cheese mixture into the pastry case and return to the oven. Bake in the oven for 35–40 minutes, or until just set. If it begins to brown or swell, open the oven door for 2 minutes, then reduce the temperature to 120°C/250°F/Gas Mark ½ and leave the tart to cool in the oven. Chill in the refrigerator until cold. Decorate and serve with fresh raspberries.

Try this: FOR AN ALTERNATIVE: 338 FOR A MAIN MEAL: 340

Tiramisu

SERVES 4

225 g/8 oz mascarpone
   cheese
25 g/1 oz icing sugar, sifted
150 ml/¼ pint strong brewed
   coffee, chilled

300 ml/½ pint double cream
3 tbsp coffee liqueur
125 g/4 oz Savoiardi or
   sponge finger biscuits
50 g/2 oz plain dark

chocolate, grated or made
   into small curls
cocoa powder, for dusting
assorted summer berries,
   to serve

Lightly oil and line a 900 g/2 lb loaf tin with a piece of clingfilm. Put the mascarpone cheese and icing sugar into a large bowl and using a rubber spatula, beat until smooth. Stir in 2 tablespoons of chilled coffee and mix thoroughly.

Whip the cream with 1 tablespoon of the coffee liqueur until just thickened. Stir a spoonful of the whipped cream into the mascarpone mixture, then fold in the rest. Spoon half of the the the mascarpone mixture into the prepared loaf tin and smooth the top.

Put the remaining coffee and coffee liqueur into a shallow dish just bigger than the biscuits. Using half of the biscuits, dip one side of each biscuit into the coffee mixture, then arrange on top of the mascarpone mixture in a single layer. Spoon the rest of the mascarpone mixture over the biscuits and smooth the top.

Dip the remaining biscuits in the coffee mixture and arrange on top of the mascarpone mixture. Drizzle with any remaining coffee mixture. Cover with clingfilm and chill in the refrigerator for 4 hours.

Carefully turn the tiramisu out on to a large serving plate and sprinkle with the grated chocolate or chocolate curls. Dust with cocoa powder, cut into slices and serve with a few summer berries.

Try this: FOR AN ALTERNATIVE: 344 FOR A MAIN MEAL: 128

Index